The Lost Tribes OF POP

Goths, Folkies, iPod Twits and Other Musical Stereotypes

Tom Cox

PORTRAIT

ACKNOWLEDGEMENTS

For their invaluable support, hard work, enthusiasm, inspiration, talent and confidence boosts, I would like to thank Stacey Earley (The Defensive Eclectic), Edie Mullen (The Erudite Poptimist), Albert DePetrillo (The Emancipated Soft Rocker), Simon Trewin (The New Romantic Beach Boy) and Caspar Llewellyn-Smith (The Bluesman of North London). You are The Lost Tribes of Tom!

Visit the Portrait website!

PORTRAIT

Portrait publishes a wide range of non-fiction, including biography, history, science, music, popular culture and sport.

Visit our website to:
- read descriptions of our popular titles
- buy our books over the internet
- take advantage of our special offers
- enter our monthly competition
- learn more about your favourite Portrait authors

VISIT OUR WEBSITE AT www.portraitbooks.com

First published in 2006 by **Portrait**
an imprint of Piatkus Books Ltd
5 Windmill Street
London W1T 2JA
e-mail: info@piatkus.co.uk

*A catalogue record for this book is
available from the British Library*

ISBN 0 7499 5106 0

Data manipulation by Phoenix Photosetting, Chatham, Kent
Printed and bound in Italy by Lego SpA, Vicenza

INTRODUCTION

IT IS A complicated time to be a music fan. Then again, perhaps we should ask ourselves, when has it *not* been? Loving popular music has never been simply about loving popular music. There has always been more to it than that. If music didn't come with cultural and personal baggage, it would mean that we didn't quite love it enough. Whether it meant backcombing your hair, Johnny Cash-style, in the fifties, rejecting the clean-cut Beatles for those nasty Rolling Stones in the sixties or just growing up in the seventies and deciding that David Cassidy scared you slightly with his 'overt' sexuality and that you'd rather listen to Donny Osmond, we have always made a statement about who we are with the records we own. We might fool ourselves that we are the kind of people who can just listen and go, but even the least image-conscious and most self-assured among us are sending out a little message to the world every time we hand over our credit card at HMV, every time, even, that we choose not to turn off a song on the radio.

What we can say for sure is that the battle lines used to be a bit more clearly drawn. Back in the mists of time, it was possible to be much more definite about your musical allegiances. If you greased up your hair and wore a leather jacket, it was unlikely that you spent a lot of time socialising with fans of the Who on mopeds. If you wore safety pins in your T-shirt a few years later, pogoed and spat a lot, it was generally safe to say your best mate was not a bearded man called Star Dappled Leaf who rhapsodised about the time he shared a smoke with one of Crosby, Stills and Nash. Similar, albeit less rigid, assumptions could be made about the musical tribes of the eighties and nineties (new romantics wore excessive make-up and tended to like Spandau Ballet or Duran Duran, but not both; alternative grungy types tended to shelter from the dance-music revolution under long mops of unwashed hair; people bought the Mr Blobby single in deferred recovery from severe childhood traumas), but the Internet and the reshaping of the music industry mean that we now live in a more fragmented age of musical fandom. With every form of music so readily available and the old notion of 'underground' virtually redundant, forging an identity for yourselves via your stereo or iPod has become that much more difficult.

You might be forgiven for assuming that such an environment would breed a less interesting kind of pop consumer: not so passionate, more eclectic, less foolhardy. Indeed, during the late nineties, as illegal downloads became the norm and the music business briefly went into meltdown, there was talk of the death of the counterculture and speculation about the demise of the pop fan as we knew him/her – largely, it has to be said, by older, jaded tribes who had realised that they weren't, after all, going to change the world by the mere act of consuming their preferred sounds while (delete as applicable) getting naked in a muddy field/moshing into a close friend/staring vacantly into space and making 'big box, little box' hand movements. Such speculation has proved to be prematurely doom-laden, to say the least. In fact, the contemporary pop fan is, if anything, more colourful and entertainingly flawed than his or her predecessor – even (and often particularly) if he or she once was one of his or her predecessors. Bamboozled with more musical choice than ever and all too conscious that he or she is not the only one who has it, he or she is more desperate to impress than ever, and, as a result, more gloriously desperate to reach out to the world. The counterculture used to be buried somewhere; now its modern equivalent is all around us, swirling beautifully and improvidently.

Despite what it says on the cover of this book, I hesitate to call the 36 characters within it 'musical stereotypes'. In my dictionary, a stereotype is defined as 'an oversimplified standardised image of an idea held by one person or group of another', and I hope something more multifaceted than that is on offer here; but, since 'Goths, Folkies, iPod Twits and Other Snapshots of the Lives of Familiar Characters Who Are a Bit Like Musical Stereotypes but Not Quite' is a bit of a mouthful, I'm rolling with it. These snapshots of musical lives are the result of over a decade with one foot in the music business and two eyes all too often straying away from the stage to the people near it and those a bit further towards the sidelines. They are the result of the realisation, following several hundred interviews with musicians, that it's actually the people on the other side of the microphone who are more fun to observe. They are also the result of a lifetime of listening to music, trying a bit hard to use it as a badge of identity, then a bit hard not to, then finally realising that you can run, but you can't hide.

Some of these Tribes seem born into their musical existences. Others seem to have been led there by dark forces. Others still seem to have stumbled into them owing to a series of random, banal mishaps. Some get a little carried away, some take their record collections and MP3s a little too seriously. All of them are defined by music, in a way that they could never be defined by another art form. Why? Because music has a pliable, portable quality common to no other art form. We can make it what we want it to be (we can probably make our favourite Picasso what we want it to be as well, but we can't carry it with us everywhere we go – or not, at least, without looking like a bit of a wally). Once we have reshaped it for our own ends, music has unique persuasive powers. It can make us wind down our car window in summer and believe that others will think us deeply virile and stylish by virtue of the ringtone anthem blasting out of our Halford's-bought speakers; it can make us mould our hair into an odd, unflattering, overgelled pyramid; it can make us fall in love; it can make us buy an item of headgear we despise. If we are extremely unlucky, it can make us do all these things at once. Similar behaviour will probably continue ad infinitum. No matter how gargantuan the memories of our iPods become, no matter how hard it becomes to stage a new form of music rebellion, no matter how easy it becomes to access every song our heart desires, we will always be attempting to use music to help us find out who we really are, to pretend to be someone else, to make us what we want to be, to get into a box, to get out of a box. What follows, I hope, is a celebration of this. Not a comprehensive overview of early twentieth-century music fan culture, perhaps, but a visit to some recognisable sorts caught up hopelessly in the thick of it.

Long may they stay there!

Tom Cox, 2006

THE VIRGIN GIGGER

'Do you, like, have to stage dive and stuff?' asks Margot.
'Is it easy? Do you think these pigtails are OK?'

IT'S THE FIRST night of the Patio tour and, as Margot returns from the toilet, adjusting her shirt and waving excitedly as she walks across the dance floor, Ellie notices, for the first time, something a little strange around her midriff. 'Margs, why are you wearing three belts?' she asks her friend, handing her back her suspiciously weighty can of Red Stripe. 'I don't know. I just thought it would be kind of cool,' she replies. 'Why? Are people looking at me? It's … all right, isn't it?'

Already, Margot is starting to act a little too much as if Patio were 'her' band for Ellie's liking. Only two weeks ago, before Ellie burned her the CDR of their stuff, she'd never heard of them, and certainly hadn't heard of Sid, their splint-thin, elegantly wasted lead singer. 'What would you do if you were just walking past the back of the venue, and you saw him? Sid – I mean? You'd faint, wouldn't you?' she'd asked in the back of Ellie's dad's Renault Espace on the way here. Ellie's older brother, Adam, was in the front seat at the time, his back to both of them, but Ellie could see the muscles in his neck move, as he aimed his eyes heavenwards. It's not that she doesn't appreciate having a new gig-going buddy. She just wishes Margot could cool it a bit, and stop asking so many questions. 'Do you, like, have to stage dive and stuff?' 'Is it easy?' 'Do you think these pigtails are OK?' 'Do you think we'll be the youngest there?' It's not surprising that, as soon as they arrived in the venue, Adam made himself scarce. 'He's off to interview the support band, for the college paper,' explained Ellie, in the foyer. 'No way! Really? He's talking to Generation Zed!' Margot shouted, causing a girl with a Bettie Page haircut ahead of them in the queue to raise an eyebrow and smirk at her boyfriend. Margot has no idea who Generation Zed are but she has seen their name and logo on a poster for tonight's gig, and is sure they must be great. After all, why wouldn't they be, if they're supporting Patio?

The first thing that Margot notices about tonight is all the logos on the T-shirts. Immediately, upon walking into the venue, she became self-conscious about her £8.99 'Total Hottie' top from Dorothy Perkins's sale rack. Was it the wrong choice? Who exactly *are* the Arcade Fire? And was that disdain that she caught in the eye of the girl with the nose stud, as she checked out Margot's Claire's Accessories wristbands? All these concerns start to fade slightly, however, as, finally – a full twenty minutes late! – the headline attraction take the stage.

Although she would never admit it to Ellie, who is now a veteran of the Bournemouth live scene (tonight is her fifth gig, in total), the first few songs seem ridiculously loud to Margot; it's hard to pick out the tunes she's spent the last fortnight learning to love. Nevertheless, she finds herself carried away by the energy, and, while she experiments with a variety of different post-song celebrations, another part of her is taking notes on her surroundings, seeing how this new habitat can help her turn into the person she's been waiting to become since buying her first fake tattoo. After each of the first five songs, she turns to Ellie to enthuse into her ear, in the way that those around her seem to be doing, but finds it difficult to do so without showering her friend's neck with spittle. By the end, she has settled for a cool, insouciant kind of applause, in imitation of the cool girls to the left of the stage. They look as if they're from London, and will probably get to meet Sid later.

Margot finds it hard to make out what her hero is mumbling about between songs, but she knows it must be profound. A few days ago, as she ate wild-mushroom risotto in the living room with her parents, she watched him being interviewed by that boring political Scottish woman – Kirsty someone, the one that her dad fancies – and found it hard to believe that someone so sensitive and intelligent could be part of the same gender as the boys in school. It had been nice of her dad to record the programme for her, but slightly less nice for him to go on about how 'wet' Sid was the whole way through it. 'You're just threatened,' she told him, as Sid spoke gently and eloquently about his beautiful dreams. Then she left the room, partly because she was starting to blush, and partly because she wanted to go and find her dictionary and look up what 'Arcadia' was. One night soon, when her mum and dad are in bed, she'll watch the whole thing again, properly. She could probably do it tonight. Why not? Sure, she's got the youth-orchestra trip tomorrow, but at the moment she feels as if she could stay awake for ever. As she and Ellie and Adam wait for the Renault under a bright lamppost in the car park, the two girls sharing a pack of Trebor Softmints, she looks uniquely alive. If Ellie's really honest, even she, yawning as the night's proceedings play themselves out predictably, notices the light in her friend's eyes. It's still there as they drop her off twenty minutes later. Two of the belts, however, seem to have mysteriously disappeared.

THE MORBID FUTURIST

How does Kurt spend his money? Nobody is quite sure.

THE DEFINING MOMENT in Kurt's life came in June 1985. Of course, if you were one of the few people who had been privileged enough to get familiar with his minimalist assortment of possessions, you might have guessed this, having come across a DAT of his intriguingly titled, unfinished tone-poem epic, *June 1985: The Serpentine Periphery*. But you would also know that this period remains a forbidden topic of conversation. Those who have kept in touch with Kurt since then – just two or three, all of whom remain fiercely loyal, yet exasperatingly distant from their synthesiser-loving friend – can now only dimly recall the young, relatively carefree Kurt, with his love of early Cure and Cabaret Voltaire.

Only a trace of his naïve aestheticism remains, beneath the dark cloud of modern Kurt, with his uniformly black and grey Muji wardrobe, unchanging rectangular hair and inexplicable obsession with signal processors.

So what went wrong? You might have written it off as a bit of ordinary, unrequited, late adolescent love, if you hadn't seen the way Kurt's eyes burned when he first looked across the lecture room. Her name was Greta, and he will never forget the way time seemed to stop as her pale, turtle-necked form made its unyielding way up to the lectern to collect her freshly marked paper on 'Production of Meaning in the Modernist Era'. 'Go on!' urged his friends. 'Ask her out!' But he had to wait to fine-tune the compilation tape he was making for her, had to get his Ultravox segueing seamlessly into his David Sylvian – by which point she'd gone off with a bloke called Tez, who wore white socks with slip-on loafers and looked like one of Bucks Fizz.

That was then and this is now – and 'now', in Kurt's head, will forever be a futuristic apocalyptic state where the guitar has been outlawed, the sun doesn't shine and Breuer Wassily chairs are standard. A bit like the scene on the roof in *Blade Runner*, but without the feel-good factor. There have been other women in Kurt's life (each of whom has attempted to undermine his stark, perfectionist approach to home furnishing with the liberal spreading of scatter cushions), but he's never really recovered from that first, unrequited love. Instead, those who attempt to befriend or love him, while at first intrigued by his dark countenance and hardwood floors, will tend to be pushed away – not only by his abrupt, precise manner of speaking, but also by his habit of listening to recordings of the inner workings of submarines and claiming that the Pet Shop Boys would have been better if they'd just been Chris on his own, without Neil. Occasionally, a fellow futurist will roll up at his warehouse flat, wondering if he wants to catch a gig by John Foxx or a re-formed

Erasure, only to find him lost in a pensive mood, attempting to disembowel a 1970s telephone.

How does Kurt spend his money? Nobody is quite sure. Despite being handsomely remunerated for designing state-of-the-art office blocks for some of the giants of European information technology, he still seems to own very little of value, if you ignore his four interlinked Roland keyboards, his £3,000 futon and his five identical black overcoats. He doesn't take drugs – or at least not since one night in 1991 (a night that remains an embarrassment to him but an endless, cheering revelation to his closest friends) when he took his first and only E – and his approach to dining is a frugal one. 'I did not have the olives,' he will announce, as, in record time, he divides the restaurant bill for the meal he has shared with seven colleagues. He sees nothing odd about this, just as he sees nothing odd in interrupting some healthy small talk by announcing, apropos of nothing, 'I have some of the happiest moments of my life in airport departure lounges,' or talking about the album he plans to make about the secret thoughts of plants. Occasionally, a musically savvy client will think he's got the measure of him and try to get him into a conversation about Human League, *Lodger*-era David Bowie or Lou Reed, only to find *Dare* written off as a compromise of the purity of Phil Oakey's earlier vision, the entire oeuvre of the Thin White Duke dismissed as 'plagiaristic pandering' and *Metal Machine Music* described as 'sweet, but fundamentally too melodic'. His goodbyes will be economical – God help those who attempt an air kiss! – and he will make his way off into the night quickly, whether he's being put up in a fancy hotel in a far-off land, or just going back to his flat in Southampton, the city where he was born and has lived all his life. 'Did you see that German guy?' a waitress will ask her colleague, as she picks up the most precise tip of the month and watches Kurt's geometrically neat form disappear out of the establishment. 'He was kind of weird, but kind of sexy as well.'

THE OLD FOLKIE

Jean remembers the good old days clearly, of course.
Pentangle at the Roundhouse, or was it the Marquee?

IT'S A DIGNIFIED way to grow old, being a folk survivor. Too few people acknowledge that, thought Jean's daughter, Emma, the other day. Sometimes, on her rare trips beyond the walled garden of her cottage in Stow on the Wold, Jean herself might quite easily think the same thing, but she's too nice and selfless for that. By the herbs section at Waitrose she'll often notice the musical casualties of her generation: greasy men with comb-overs and Hendrix T-shirts, former Marianne Faithfulls who've injudiciously kept the faith in the hippie dream. To her, they're just former young people. To Emma, they're walking catastrophes. Jean, like them, listens to the same music she listened to at 20. The difference is that it seems to suit her long grey hair and the ivy growing up her wall as well as it once suited her tie-died T-shirt and barren, freezing urban bedsit.

Gentle sounds, weird sounds, timeless sounds, pastoral sounds: they're still all with her, meticulously catalogued – 'I love your handwriting,' her late husband Colin always used to say to her – on the tapes she keeps next to the rickety tape recorder in her kitchen. They say they wear out after a few hundred plays, but hers are all serving her well after more than that, so she's never felt the need to go digital, just as she's never felt the need to sell her Vauxhall Viva or update her black-and-white TV, made by Bush in 1976. Besides, the whirring and muffled dustiness somehow seems to complement John Martyn's 'Spencer the Rover'.

She remembers the good old days clearly, of course. Pentangle at the Roundhouse, or was it the Marquee? Some bloke wearing a horse's head mask. His mate apparently lost in an entirely different place in his head, singing a song to himself – something about 'the starving earth' and 'the reaper'. Good strong face, he had, if you got rid of the Jethro Tull beard. Then came the eighties: the wire-cutting at Greenham Common, the CND events – a toddling Emma smearing a custard pie in the face of a man in a Maggie Thatcher mask – and babies, so many babies, especially on camping holidays in Devon with the gang. Then, when the babies were old, cats – seven, at the last count, though Emma isn't entirely convinced that her mum hasn't sneakily lured another couple away from her neighbours with some of her legendary on-the-bone ham.

'Do you think I should get my hair cut?' Jean asks as they weed around some hollyhocks in the yard. Emma, who can't remember her mum visiting a hairdresser in the 29 years she's known her, is shocked. 'No!' she says – a reaction that comes from instinct rather than careful consideration. She has to admit that it is a problem in Jean's cottage, hair. Gets everywhere, no matter how often she comes round and helps clean up, and it's recently occurred to Emma that not all of it might come from Mr Plops, Osiris, Ponsenby, Rattlebone, Prudence, Zeus and Delawney. She worries about her mum, especially now there's a new man on the scene, John, an antiques dealer from the other end of town, whom Jean met while buying a 1940s corn-dolly windmill. Seems nice enough, but what will he think of the living space Emma has come to refer to (only in the presence of her husband, Ian, mind) as 'the malthouse', or Jean's spellbooks, or the ever-present copy of James George Frazer's *The Golden Bough* by the bed, or the pong-ridden mobile recycling unit that the Vauxhall Viva has become? On one hand, she worries about her mum becoming the local Lonely Cat Woman in a decade's time, gibbering to herself and going to the shops in her slippers. On the other hand, what if John's only in it to get his hands on Jean's 200-year-old po cabinet? Jean watches her worrying about all these things. 'Silly girl,' she thinks, wondering whether she played that song about a man stealing your time to her a little too much in the seventies. 'I'll just make him some jam, and see how it goes.' Everything will be fine. And, if it isn't, there'll still be Sandy Denny, the hollyhocks and several warm bundles of fur to cuddle up to at night – just as always.

THE iPOD TWIT

*Charlie spends more time loading up his iPod
than actually listening to it.*

THE GIRL WITH the ethnic bag and the nose stud has barely set leather-free foot into the carriage but already Charlie has clocked her through his Cutler and Gross glasses. It's just human nature, he thinks, as he recalls a conversation that took place in the Soho Slug and Lettuce last year, where three of his mates – Drew, Smitho and the Jinxster – admitted to selecting tube and train seats almost entirely on the basis of how many desirable women were sitting nearby. Obviously, it's easier when it's the other way around and he's the one entering the carriage, but, as long as he adopts a faraway look and makes certain his bright, white headphones are visible, he knows there's a good chance the girls will be drawn to him – particularly at a quiet time like this, when the only other two people in the carriage have nose beards. The scarf helps, too. On a mild day in April, it gives you an air of delicate complexity, he feels.

From here, it's usually all a formality. Twenty minutes south of Edinburgh, without looking up, he'll ask, 'What are you studying?' She'll be off her guard and grateful. Soon, he'll be showing her his Folk, his Garage, his Reggae. Then it will be on to the subgenres: 'Acid Chill', 'Kettlecore', 'Electro-Spittle', 'Pedigree Chum'. 'I made a lot of them up myself,' he'll say, puffing his chest out, yet slipping further down in his chair, roughly at the time the Intercity 125 reaches Doncaster. Then he'll outline his intention eventually to live in New Zealand in a little too much detail. Before he changes at Peterborough and heads across country to his parents' mock-Tudor home, he'll have her number. It will be deliberately incorrect, but he will have it.

He's had his iPod for three months, now – the model with the maximum memory capacity, obviously – during which time he's spent more time loading it up than actually listening to it. With everything from Beyoncé to Abbess Hildegard of Bingen's 'A Feather on the Breath of God' on there, he views his eclecticism less as a feature of his personality and more as an impressive extra body part that he can nonchalantly wave around in front of strangers. When he's doing this, he can often sound like a sound bite from the front section of a style magazine. 'These things are revolutionising the way we own and store music,' he tells the girl on the train, a pottery student from Northampton called Karen. She nods as if she's listening, but what she's wondering is why he speaks in that weird languid way. Is it because he's posh? Why does he look at her as if she were a mirror? And how old is he? She can't quite work it out. He seems like a student, but more boring, too – and sort of more stupid, now she comes to think of it. Shouldn't he be working in the City or something?

In reality, Charlie left university a couple of years ago. Since then, he's been doing a bit of this, a bit of that – finance-related stuff, mainly, arranged by his Scottish uncle Archie, 'the dark horse of the family'. His degree's in marine biology, a field he assumes is not much use in Edinburgh (not that he's bothered to check). But, despite what the Jinxster and the rest of the Berkshire Bad Boys say, he's not going to move back down south just yet. Like everything else with Charlie, there's no hurry. 'It's just big-fish, small-pond syndrome, what you've got, my man!' the Jinx said, and Charlie laughed it off, but knew there was something in it. He still remembers that day in Caffé Nero, where he unveiled 'The Pod', which he has pet-named Ivan. Sociology majors with too much eye-shadow milled around.

'What's that, Handsome Charles?' said Melissa, one of the *baristas*, as she stroked the menu wheel, relishing the little clicking sounds. He loved that glowing feeling of easy power, when you can just tell someone really, really fancies you. In the next three hours, she couldn't keep away from his seat – returned at least three times, to see if he wanted anything else. He even made her his own playlist, told her about the little pink version she could get. But he'll wait. She can make the first move – just like this one, Karen. She's gone a bit distant now, so he probably won't get his copy of Jack Kerouac's *Big Sur* out just yet. He probably won't call her, either. What's important is the number itself: another triumph. He'll show it to the BB Boys in the Slug tonight – number 74 this year, stored right there on Ivan itself. Later, he'll tell a story about what a great breakdancer he used to be, but, when the Jinxster challenges him to do a butterfly or a backspin, he'll decline, as ever, claiming he doesn't want to get his artfully turned-up jeans dirty.

RETRO MAN

*It's not so much that Terry ignores modern life and more
that modern life doesn't seem to exist while he's around.*

AS THE RAC van pulls off the bumpy road and judders to a halt, its
driver takes a moment to register fully the spectacle in front of him.
He's acted as the automotive saviour of all sorts in his time, as he will
tell you on a Friday night in the Dog and Gown, but now, looking at
the miserable-looking man with the rounded spectacles and shaggy yet
symmetrical hair – strangely evocative of a pair of inverted commas –
and his tiny Japanese girlfriend, sitting on the kerb, he's surprised and
not a little unnerved. There are no two ways about it: this isn't the kind
of thing you see every day on the A65, just south of Kirby Lonsdale.

Terry is used to this sort of reaction by now. His more creative,
musically literate friends back in Plaistow might say he looks like one

of the Move or the Creation, but get into the outside world and it's Lennon, Lennon, Lennon. The unimaginativeness of the generation he romanticises, as they move into their dotage, never ceases to amaze him. He can see what his rescuer is thinking on this cold, windy night, as he takes in the flares, the kaftan and poor, shivering Miyu, on his right. Provided he doesn't call her 'Yoko', they'll deal with this stoically, as usual. It's the second time that the Morris Traveller has broken down during the holiday, the fourth time this year, and it's the same every time. These middle-aged men – these proper men, with their rough hands and hunter-gatherer skills – probably think Terry's a bit wet for calling them out just to mend a flat tyre, and he knows they're right: he feels like a fraud, a truly modern masculine failure, at times like these. But on another level he enjoys their confusion, their inability to place him in the scheme of modern youth, their bafflement at why someone young enough to be their son would dress in the kind of clothes that they long ago dismissed as laughable, and choose to drive such an unreliable car, the most elementary part of whose inner workings they have no intention of ever grappling with. Taking this into account, it's perhaps easier to understand why they grip onto his least favourite Beatle like a piece of comprehensible cultural driftwood in a sea of confusion.

The world of pop fandom is a place rife with gaping chasms between self-image and outside perception. The gap, in Terry's case, is as large as many. The difference is a stubborn awareness on his part. He knows the vast majority of the rest of the world sees him as a novelty, a walking waxwork, but that doesn't stop him believing he's a crusader for something pure and forgotten. His biweekly trips to London's Berwick Street, accompanied by Miyu – whom he originally met when they bumped shoulders while simultaneously making a beeline for a rare mod album in Reckless Records – aren't just about finding forgotten tunes to enjoy: they're also about building an impregnable retro force field around his personality. It's not so much that Terry ignores modern life and, more, that modern life doesn't seem to exist while he's around. The more immersed he feels in the past, the better he feels about himself. This extends to clothes, too, and it's one of his many points of pride that he hasn't bought a single 'outer' garment of a non-second-hand nature since 1992. The occasional compromise does, however, have to be made, and every time he buys a new pair of underpants from Marks & Spencer he feels a small part of him dying.

What does Terry do for a living? His friends, all of whom also have vast collections of original sixties and seventies vinyl and many of whom also have Japanese girlfriends, find it hard to say. They're always bumping into him and Miyu in some north London charity shop or other – though not Oxfam, which has 'gone rubbish' since it started employing proper dealers to price up its stuff – of an afternoon, which also prompts the question, how do Terry's mates have so much spare time, too? They're getting into their mid-thirties now, but all of them seem to be either on the dole, or working part-time in record shops, or in bands who have been about to break big since Alan McGee was the chief employer of men sporting Brian Jones hairstyles. Somehow, though, the future still manages to appear bright. Together, they hunch, mutton-chop sideburns almost touching, in smoky, dusty pubs in need of a refurbishment, and beside market stalls, complimenting one another on the yokes on their new cowboy shirts, using the word 'yeah' 17 times per sentence, and enthusing about an upcoming gig by the reformed Moody Blues, whose early seventies stuff is 'well underrated'. Only a few yards away, a loud teenager with no colour co-ordination is talking to someone called 'Becka' on a mobile phone and a fat-bottomed, spoiler-heavy car is pumping out ugly, apocalyptic, low-register sounds, but there's the sense that, if they can just huddle together and keep nodding at one another, they can preserve what they have. One day, they might get proper jobs, raise families, belatedly decide that, actually, 'Some Girls' by Rachel Stevens is a really good song, but, for now, with just a little commitment, it is 1971 for ever.

THE PR GIRL

Tabby is, quite possibly, the oldest 28-year-old in London.

AS THE TWELVE-legged train of shuffling denim and casual trainers enters the pub, the band and the journalist hang back and Tabby catches the barman's eye with a look that means business, one that communicates that beneath the ostensible hostess-with-the-mostest manner, beneath the CBGB vampire chic, she, just like him, is a worker of the night, not here for fun. She doesn't have to ask anyone what their tipple is twice. Memorising rounds of drinks of all sizes comes as second nature when you've played chaperone to a dozen mummy's-boy music scribes on a junket to New York, when you've cruised through Rio de Janeiro with two of Britain's loudest, least hygienic rock bands, when every day you speak to 60 different people as if they were your best friend. She gets her receipt, as always, and makes the introductions. Afterwards, she moves away, turning her attention to the six voicemail messages that have accumulated on the taxi ride here, all of which she has not previously been able to listen to, for fear of hurting the feelings of Biff, the lead singer of Colossal Worm, who has been lost in a monologue about an out-of-body experience in the Mojave Desert. She will probably get a chance to return the two most important ones – the reviewer from *Q* magazine who can't get into the venue, the photographer from the *Independent* who wants to know how the band would feel about recreating the cover of Abbey Road in the 20-minute slot she has been allocated for tomorrow morning – before Biff or one of his henchman asks her to get him a falafel-and-hummus wrap. The guy from the *Highbury and Islington Express* will just have to wait.

It's weird. She has made a success of her life, moved to the capital city, left small-minded acquaintances behind, yet she feels, these days, as if she is constantly surrounded by the boys she would never have taken a second look at at school. Fifteen years ago, Biff (or his equivalent) would have been picking up bits of gravel-caked sandwich from the playground floor while she compared lip gloss with her friends and mooned at Nick Henshaw, the coolest guy in fourth-year business studies (and the destroyer of said sandwich). Now, he acts like royalty and she acts as his surrogate mother – or nanny, at the very least (it's the journalists who really need the mothering). She used to think there was some kind of justice to this: the way that the Nick Henshaws of this world ended up in dead-end jobs in Tamworth and Darley Dale, fitting objects that made their hands greasy and reliving the good old days of the PE changing room in the Gown and Whippet, while their geeky nemeses got the record contracts and the jobs freelancing for the music monthlies. More recently, she hasn't been so sure. If there's one thing worse than a nerd scrambling around in the dirt, it's a nerd whose ego has been boosted out of all proportion to reality by the proximity of famous people and a few misguided, adoring teenage girls.

It is quite possible that Tabby is the oldest 28-year-old in London. In eight years in the industry, she has seen everything she needs to see to know exactly what kind of business she's in and what her function is within it. She's heard the story about the blow job that was exchanged for the good review, about the journo who got his mate to review the gig. She's seen the wannabes with the cigarettes in their cleavage come and go, heard them so pleased with themselves for finding their own line ('I know I'm paid to say this, but when I say this record is the most transcendental thing you'll hear this year, I mean it …'), seen them let temptation get in their way – whether it be the promo cupboard or the in-house pusherman (a happy-go-lucky Rastafarian Brummie from reception called Rod, whom she frequently chats to about *Gardeners' Question Time*, to the bewilderment of her more cred-conscious colleagues). She also knows enough to realise what the more 'specialised' areas of the music industry say behind her back. 'When you go to bed at night, where is it, exactly, that you tell yourself your skills lie?' said one particularly spiteful hack, who had been denied an interview with a leading soul diva at the last moment. Her talent might lie in the muddy area of being 'good with people', but she knows, in her heart of hearts, that that is often something to be more proud of than the talents required for other, more respected areas of the professional world she lives in. Has an A&R man ever had the indignity of being made to cry, as a 20-year-old, in the hallway outside the *NME* by a reviews editor, then had to pick himself up, travelling one floor upwards in the elevator, and tout his product around a rival, equally acerbic, PR-unfriendly music weekly? Has a record company website designer ever had – just on the off chance of getting a record reviewed – cheerfully to chat up the answerphone of a man who, only two days previously, had asked them unseemly questions about the colour of their underwear? And, yes, so what if she makes little notes about the private lives of the journalists who are nice enough to take her calls – a bout of flu here, a new gym membership there – to help her along her gregarious way? You might call it phoney. She calls it survival. And the truth is, when people are civil, she really does still enjoy the dialogue. When she says, 'How are you?' she genuinely wants to know.

She'll be out again with the band tomorrow. It will give her phone ear a rest, at least. The *Abbey Road* plan? Sounds like a bit of cliché, but she'll say, 'Great idea!' and do her best to facilitate it. She'll bring drinks and very specific types of filled ciabatta to every member of Colossal Worm except their bassist, Warren, an elfish, silent type who never seems to eat anything and just sits in the corner applying mascara. As thanks for this, she will be permitted to hear their moaning conversations about the music business and 'The Man'. Is she part of this amorphous gentleman? She supposes so. After all, it's not as if Biff and co. talked to her like a woman or anything. No doubt, they'll be whingeing even more in a couple of years' time when, after they have drunk the record company dry, they find themselves without a deal. Tabby will still be there, though – even wiser, if that's possible. But she won't be there for ever. She's already got her eye on a couple of Open University courses. It's looking like a toss-up between landscape gardening and ancient art history. After all, she wouldn't want to end up like Kitty, the head of PR. She gets goose pimples when she looks in the woman's eyes. Rumour has it she hasn't been the same since she slept with one of Ned's Atomic Dustbin in 1991.

LOCAL BAND BLOKE

*'We've signed this new band called Andy Smith's Pink Fridge,' says Gavin.
'Like Coldplay meets Green Day but with a lesbian singer.'*

LUCY RECOGNISES GAVIN from the moment she walks into the reception, but it's not until he's launched into the evening's third rendition of 'Mustang Sally' that she manages to place him. As he gurns and bellows in a manner that owes a little more to that fat bloke from the Commitments than he'd like to admit, she takes his half-bleached bald man's buzz cut in her mind's eye and replaces it with dried-out, flying Miles Hunt curls, swaps the sensible slacks for frayed camouflage pants. Suddenly, it's 1992 again, she's standing outside the Norwich branch of HMV, clutching the new Kingmaker single as if it were a wartime food stamp, and her mate, Nicky, is pointing out the bloke who owns a record label. 'What, him?' she is saying, looking at Gav. 'But he's only about twenty or something. Wow!'

'So what did happen to the label?' she asks him 20 minutes later, back in the twenty-first century, as the wedding guests stumble back to their cars. 'Oh, it's still going,' he says, as he wheels a speaker stack across the linoleum. 'We've signed this new band called Andy Smith's Pink Fridge? Have you heard them? They're da bomb. Like Coldplay meets Green Day but with a lesbian singer? I've got a feeling this is going to be the year when it really happens for the indies. People are starting to get bored with all that chart shit.' Then he's telling her about Saccharine Ninny, and about how they broke up when Mike fell for some bird, the big wuss, but how the band's still together, in a way, but now it's called Love Puddle and much more industrial-sounding, and they just got asked to do a support at a freshers' ball in Hull. And for a moment she catches herself genuinely wanting to remember or even find out who the hell Mike is, but then she thinks about that episode of *Friends* – the one where Monica hooks up for a date with the coolest guy in her old high school, then finds out he's still *exactly* like he was at high school. 'So what do you do, these days?' Gavin asks her, finally.

'Oh, I live in Manchester and lecture in language and communication in the School of Psychological Sciences at the university.'

'Cool. So you're back in town for a few days? I don't know if you're doing anything tomorrow night but Love Puddle are playing the Cider Shed in Shepperton St Faith. Not covers like tonight. I'm talking the real shiznit. This just pays the rent. I'm going to jack it in soon, actually.'

Half an hour later, back in the van, Gavin pinches himself sharply on the neck, which is his wont when he's looking back on the day's events and chiding himself for social indiscretions, adding to a patch of red blotches frequently mistaken for shaving rash.

Damn! He knew he should have offered to put her on the guest list – or 'the guestie', as he refers to it – for the Shed gig. Oh, well. It's not as if there's much room or anything, what with the list already running to two pages and including Jim's mum and dad and Ian's new girlfriend Wendy, and Terry and Jean, that nice couple who run the garden centre who everyone says don't wear underwear, and Colin, the bloke from the local paper, who's blown him out the last couple of times but who said he'd definitely be there this time, wouldn't miss it for the world.

'Fancy a stop at Burger Queen?' he calls to Jim, the drummer for Love Puddle, who aren't actually called Love Puddle tonight, but A Few Good Men, which is their wedding-gig name. 'Burger Queen' is what Gavin calls Burger King. He also calls Borders 'Margins', Top Man 'Bottom Woman' and River Island 'Lake Country' (although, in his heart of hearts, even he admits the last one is not one of his strongest slices of wordplay). Jim, whose surname is Newlove, kind of laughed when Gavin called him 'Oldhate', the first five or six times, but it soon started to annoy him. Only slightly less annoying is his new habit of using urban slang to describe white-boy indie rock.

For the umpteenth time, Gavin's thoughts return to last summer, the sole time Colin, the local paper guy, came to see Love Puddle. 'Yeah!' he said, afterwards, in the dressing room, when Gavin asked him what he thought. 'Yeah!' Sure, he didn't say he enjoyed it, but when someone smiles a lot and says 'Yeah!', that means they've had a good time, doesn't it? Such a pisser that the review got knocked off the page by that story about the Christmas lights fundraiser and the kid with Crohn's disease. Still – it was probably for the best, in the long run. A lot's clicked into place since then, sonically speaking. And, now he comes to think of it, Ian's idea for the band all to get matching parkas in the Next sale might not have been the best move in the world, image-wise. You learn from these things and you get stronger. You learn that it takes time to find yourself. You learn that it doesn't matter if the bloke from Q magazine sends back your fourth demo with the seal still intact and, even when you lay off the cheeseburgers for a full two months, your cheekbones still look like those of a greedy plumber. It's as Gavin was saying to Gloria, the cashier in the post office, the other day, when he was buying his copy of *Wordsearch* magazine and renewing his road tax: this isn't the sixties any more; we know that this rock game is for life. 'I know what you mean,' she replied. 'You only have to look at that James Blunt boy! He didn't make it until he was twenty-eight!'

And, OK, so Gav did surreptitiously try to hide his date of birth on his driving licence as she said it, but he could see that she saw him as someone young, someone who was going against the grain. And Lucy, too: getting on for a decade and a half since he'd last seen her, and, when he told her how he could feel good times were coming and that the world was opening up to Love Puddle, there was that look – that one that made him feel vital and loose, the one that made it all worthwhile. You think he would still get that look if he'd got a job in a solicitor's office, or as the manager of Commercial Slut Megastore, or as an accountant? You might think so, but, if you did, you'd be living in a dream world.

THE LINE DANCER

*According to Pauline, line dancing was just
written in the stars for some folk.*

THERE COMES A time when every woman must face the fact that
she's too old for the world of mainstream nightclubbing, and for
Pauline that time came shortly after her 38th birthday. She was
starting to see Blackpool deteriorate. Where there'd been just three
puddles of vomit outside the Waterfront on an average Saturday
night back in the day, now there tended to be between 10 and 14,
and for some reason those men you saw standing on the street
wearing fake comedy breasts just weren't quite connecting with the
funny bone any more. She'll always remember the date when she
started to indulge in what remains, after bingo, the UK's second

most popular recreational activity – 19 May 2002 – because it was exactly 10 years, to the day, after the original release of Billy Ray Cyrus's 'Achy Breaky Heart'. Not that she knew that at the time, of course, but now she realises just how spooky the whole thing is, and, should you give her half a chance, she will be quick to tell you so, over a bottle of Newcastle Brown Ale. '*Bloody* spooky,' she will whisper, leaning in close to your face and spraying a little hot saliva in your earlobe.

The only way to explain it is the theory put forward by her mate Mac, that line dancing is just written in the stars for some folk – a theory that it takes a brave man to posit while standing outside a chippy in Lancaster. She probably should have known it back on those nights long ago at the Boardwalk – the way she used to dance that bit more exuberantly to the tunes with a twang, try that much harder to get Kel, Marie and Dosser out on the floor in some kind of synchrony. 'Cotton-Eye Joe' – that was the one she'd liked. That said, her taste is a lot more refined these days, what with the *Eighty Line Dance Favourites* box set Mac bought her for Christmas, and her Clint Black albums. Mac may seem a bit weird to people who've never met him – a bloke who's lived in Accrington all his life, talking in a Texan accent – but, if she'd never bumped into him that drunken day that she wandered into the Country and Western Store with Dosser and tried on that Stars and Stripes waistcoat for a laugh, where would she be? She'll tell you where: ordering fireman-themed stripograms for her mates and rewatching Peter Kay videos. And nobody wants that, do they?

Pauline's found this a lot in her life: the most revealing moments are those when you're half gone. It took three bottles of cheap pink champagne to realise that Mike, the used-car salesman she met at the car boot sale in Lytham, was a complete knob handle, and one more than that to realise that there are few things she likes better in life than putting on a Stetson and linking arms with a pensioner and a chakra teacher of worryingly handbag-like complexion. She would like to try the dancing itself while drunk, but worries that she might fall over while attempting to belly-roll or duck-pivot. Still, she is learning fast, particularly now the Sam and Sarah West *Carolina Shag for Beginners* DVD she ordered on import has arrived.

Why does she like line dancing? You may as well ask, 'Why does Mac have a beard?' Obviously, there was a time when he didn't have one, but now it's been forgotten and doesn't really count – it was just an intermediary period on the road to somewhere more definitive. It's funny: she never thought she liked bristly men, but on those occasions when the euphoria of the night's fifth perfectly executed male pull-through has set in and she flirtatiously nuzzles her nose into what he calls 'the big chin beaver', she thinks she could quite fancy him. He's not the reason she's here – she'd love the feeling of strutting her stuff to 'Islands in the Stream' in an out-of-commission school gym, whoever her chaperone was – but, equally, the North Lancashire Shaggers wouldn't quite be the same without him. She's just not sure he feels the same way, and currently finds herself vacillating between thinking he's an entirely asexual being and suspecting he's a secret swinger. True, the thrusting, outward symbols are there – the fake Winchester rifle, the 1955 T-Bird he bought on eBay and had shipped over from Denver – but why hasn't he made a move? After all, she's the youngest female Shagger by a good ten years, if you ignore Little Susie, the granddaughter of the Kesbys, who won the talent contest at Butlin's last year (and she dearly hopes Mac *does* ignore her, in *that* way). Perhaps Pauline will wait just a bit longer, then make the first move herself – maybe on the summer trip to Nashville that Mac has arranged. If he says yes, great. If he says no, she'll find a tall Southern gent and get her fun that way. Who knows? Perhaps Billy Ray will be in town.

THE LO-FI ELITIST

'Am I the only person in this city who has heard of The Sea and Cake?'
mutters Jim under his breath.

'THOSE WHO CAN'T do, teach. Those who can't teach, teach gym,' said Woody Allen. Similarly, those who can't make records for a living often sell them instead, and some of those who aren't very good at selling them end up working in second-hand record shops. Not that you would want to tell Jim this. Truffaut, his post-rock jazz-funk band, may have split up last year in the face of mass indifference from the corporate world, but he still has high hopes for his bedroom side project, Adverse Camber.

'It's kind of Suicide-meets-Edgar-Allan-Poe-meets-the-sound-of-falling-dust – best listened to with a monster doobie and a North

Carolina state of mind,' he scrawled in the covering note that he sent to the head of Domino Records, along with his demo, which was recorded in Clerkenwell, London. It's been eight weeks now, though, and there's been no word back, so for now he's still stuck behind the counter at Honest Nick's.

Jim's sales technique, now perfected, after five years in the trade, is one based more on knowledge than customer relations. Having passed Nick's legendary admittance exam with flying colours – he still thinks of naming the first 20 Fall albums, in order, sans hesitation, as one of his life's crowning achievements – and outlasted almost every one of the scruffy, inventively shaven men who have worked alongside him, he now has the freedom of the shop stereo. On a generous day, he will allow requests from customers to be played, but never for more than a minute, and not if Captain Beefheart's *Trout Mask Replica* happens to be on at the time. 'I make it my evangelical mission to listen the old "Mask of the Red Cool" at least once a day,' he said last year, during Truffaut's one and only fanzine interview. When he said the 'Mask of the Red Cool' bit, he made air quotes with his fingers.

When Jim's parents tell relatives that Jim works in a shop, they get an image of a grown-up version of the nice quiet boy who had all that trouble fitting in at school (an unfair business – it really wasn't that unusual to wear home-knitted jumpers at the age of 16, was it?), now making his way in the world, exchanging goods with a smile. Jim would be horrified by this image. It is now precisely three years and 14 days since the last time he said 'thanks' to a customer, and that came out more as 'thurplnks', owing to the fact that he was a little nervous, since the guitarist from Mogwai was browsing in the prog-rock rack at the time.

Usually, he will coolly evaluate his prey, as they bring him their soiled, sub-charity-shop Grace Jones crap, their pointless Maroon Five and ABBA commodities. Keeping eye contact to the minimum, he will go through his routine: four fingers drummed insouciantly on the counter, an invisible something picked out of his ear, a secret joke with Neil, his co-worker, then the words that have the power to strike fear into the hearts of £50 Men everywhere: 'Cash or exchange?' 'Am I the only person in this city who has heard of The Sea and Cake?' he might mutter under his breath, on a grumpy day, apropos of nothing.

During quiet periods at Nick's, when he isn't mocking Celine Dion fans that have taken a misguided turn on the way to HMV, Jim works on his novel. 'It's kind of a Stalinist reworking of Bukowski's *Post Office*, with an ironic feminist slant,' he tells Neil, ignoring a middle-aged lady who has politely enquired if he would like her to find the correct change for *The Best of Bread*. 'I've been writing it in these vast, staccato bursts, drinking shitloads of Ethiopian coffee, with Sun Ra playing in the background.' Neil wonders if this is why Jim looks so tired and dishevelled, or if that's just an impression given by his unwashed Slint T-shirt and the sparse, fluffy outcropping of hair on his chin.

At lunchtime, the two of them pop down the road for a samosa. Usually they will bump into friends from the local branch of Forbidden Planet, whom they will greet on the street with complicated handshakes that never quite seem to work, and chat that seems to consist only of the word 'yeah', repeated to the point of delirium. Such animated displays are rare. Perhaps Jim will pick up a magazine on the way back, from which he will cut out pictures to stick on the 'Evil Wall' that they keep behind the counter to set out their anti-corporate philosophy to non-believers (Elton John and Dido currently have pride of place here). Once back in the shop, he will inevitably find a civilian waiting for his collection to be priced. 'I'm really not too bothered how much you give me, I really just want to get rid of it,' the man – an insurance worker called Harry, on his lunch break – will say diplomatically, but Jim will not be rushed. As he flicks through the vinyl, he will refrain from critical comment, yet offer a succinct, devastating evaluation via a series of minuscule nostril laughs. Finally, feeling more as if he had just had his personality priced than some old albums he no longer cared for, Harry will be so grateful to leave that he will be happy to take the first price he's offered. Having escaped Jim and passed back into the outside world, he will be struck by how, despite the fact that the shop was neither smoky nor especially dusty, the outside air seems somehow much fresher than normal.

THE ROADIE

Bob honestly can't tell you how many years he's been on the road now.
His brain is too fried: not by drugs, but by sound.

IT IS A SCENE that has been repeated a billion times, in the smoky, anticipatory darkness before a billion concerts. First, a figure moseys across the stage. Momentarily, it's possible to hear a couple of thousand simultaneous intakes of breath, a rapturous spasm going through the crowd like an aural Mexican wave. 'Funny how this never gets old,' Bob thinks to himself. Head down, all business, he might look nonchalant, but he's enjoying himself, and he always sneaks a peek at the girls on the front row.

They've registered that he is not the Performer, the ripples of excitement calming into disappointment, but slowly, still savouring every moment, he picks up the Rickenbacker and strums out what's become his signature tune – a miniature, bastardised version of the opening chords to 'Highway to Hell', confirming the guitar is in tune. It has to be very, very bastardised, because it's important to keep excitement levels low, to make his employers' entrance all the more dramatic. He learned this rule a long time ago. Forgets the name of the band now. Singer used to polish the stage, drummer looked like a Muppet. Said Bob was stealing their 'thunder', they did, when he tuned up with 'Since You've Been Gone' by Rainbow. That could have been curtains for him right there, if it hadn't been for his sound-guy mate, Twiggs, vouching for him. As it happened, it was the start of a long career, which is more than he can say for the group, who, he suspects, are probably now working in KFC.

Bob honestly can't tell you how many years he's been on the road now. His brain is too fried at this point: not by drugs, but by sound. As a result of this, he is one of a unique tribe of people who can watch *The Osbournes* and think the show's patriarch is talking in perfectly intelligible English. Obviously, Ozzie is somebody he looks up to, but his real hero is Hawkwind-era Lemmy, and, although he rarely thinks about it any more, he still nurtures a perfectly formed recurring dream of joining him in a guitar duel at Brixton Academy. The dream ends with his being invited back to the room of Stacia, Hawkwind's naked dancer, who has been immobilised in her 1972 glory. Like Lemmy, Bob likes to think he's not really scared of anything, apart from snakes, whose lack of shoulders disturbs him. That said, those who know him best will tell you he has a slight thing about toothbrushes. 'There are just so many *bristles*,' he will confess, in a drunken, introverted moment.

Every Friday at 4 pm, whether he's in Hamburg, Chicago, Budapest, at home in his semi in Crewe or anywhere else, Bob calls his mum, Eileen. These calls will typically last around an hour and a half, feature a lie about his £1,000-per-month mobile-phone bill, and end with Eileen getting on Bob's nerves by worrying excessively about his nutrition. Speaking truthfully, she has a point. Wizz, one of the guys Bob met on the '95 Skynyrd reunion tour, once spread a rumour that Bob hadn't eaten a piece of fruit since Thatcher was in power. While this isn't strictly correct, he did once rejoice in the nickname 'Pastie' and doesn't feel that a night is quite complete without a chicken jalfrezi.

At the height of business, Bob and Wizz – who still often work the same crews – will talk in a language that might sound alien even to the most jargon-fixated building contractor: a grunting cacophony of 'two-by-nines', 'five nivos', and 'big-boy Ampegs'. Later, when the work's done and a crisis involving an Eventide harmoniser has been narrowly averted, the talk will turn to the good old days, as Bob and Wizz sit symbolically at the feet of Squint, the Gandalf of the West Midlands roadie scene, who worked the first Isle of Man festival and disdains any roadie who refers to himself as a 'technician'. Bob still tells friends from Crewe that nothing can be better than having a job in the hub of rock and roll, but he rarely spends any time kicking back with the musicians, and would rather retire to a nearby pub to hear one of Squint's stories any day. He knows them all by heart now. His favourite is probably the one about the Swedish festival, where the bull chewed through the cable, closely followed by the one about the guy who opened the door of the tour bus toilet at 'eighty miles per', only to find he was pissing into the fast lane of the motorway. Slightly less lucid is Squint's roadie wisdom, which will typically emerge later in the night and include sayings such as 'whores are cheap but call girls are real expensive – remember that and you'll never go wrong' and 'hard shit doesn't float, baby'. Try as he might, Bob cannot decipher how this imagery provides any sage lessons about the ins and outs of lugging amplifiers for a living, but he has found himself repeating it around some of the younger techies and getting off on the power buzz. 'No sugar on the highway tonight; no rabbits either,' he said last week to a kid in a Marilyn Manson T-shirt, who was having trouble securing some gaffer tape to a six-by-nine. The kid looked slightly confused, but seemed to take his word for it.

GLASTONBURY GIRL

Lucy used to call it 'Glasto'. She now realises that was stupid,
pretentious and childish, so calls it 'Glasters' instead.

'WHAT HAPPENED TO surrealism?' Lucy finds herself wondering
a lot these days. 'Who suddenly decided that it wasn't cool any
more, and why?' The truth is, she doesn't mind *The Mighty Boosh*
or *QI* and can catch herself humming along to Coldplay quite
frequently, but she finds herself missing those joyfully random days
of the mid-nineties, when Vic Reeves wasn't a sad old reality-TV
contestant and still said things like 'You wouldn't let it lie!' when it
was perfectly acceptable to go out with someone on the basis that
you both thought Carter the Unstoppable Sex Machine was a great
band name and that the 'How many surrealists does it take to
change a light bulb?' joke (answer: 'hairshit sprinkle witch') was the

funniest thing ever. One of the great things about Glastonbury is that all that stuff no longer seems so out of date. Suddenly, that anecdote she's been wheeling out about the 1994 festival – the one where she is standing next to the curry stall, and tells the woman next to her that her chicken is ready, only to find … it's the wrong woman! – doesn't seem so tired any more. Suddenly, she is no longer the owner of the last remaining Mega City Four T-shirt in the known universe.

Her mates have noticed this about her: she was born to breathe the Avalon air. She may bang on constantly about her list of Things You Must Do Before You Die, and make tentative plans to go white-water rafting and potholing, but her real idea of Living Life to the Full will for ever be a field in Somerset, a can of cider and the distant sound of a didgeridoo being played by a dreadlocked man called Grunf. Once she's through those gates with her new photo ID card proudly displaying her sensible bob, the transformation will begin: no longer will she be the girl who tries a little bit too hard to impress on the popbitch.com forum, the hardworking, obsessively neat girl whose love life resembles a misinterpreted Camille Paglia essay. As she puts up her tent and unpacks her vodka from her Shorn the Sheep rucksack, Susie and Gemma will take bets on what will happen first: the inevitable snog with an ageing Levellers fan, or the near-fatal fall into the edge of the campfire while trying to recreate Vic Reeves's 'chaffing' routine.

Glastonbury is never just 'Glastonbury' to Lucy. Back in the day, she used to call it 'Glasto'. She now realises that was stupid, pretentious and childish, so calls it 'Glasters' instead. She still rhapsodises about the old days – that unforgettable Saturday in 1995, when the entire eastern campsite erupted into cries of 'Bollocks!' for an hour between three and four in the morning, only to be punctuated by one lone dissenting voice quoting from a Monty Python film. Genius! Feelings of belonging don't come much stronger. Earlier in the night, Jarvis Cocker had sung 'Common

People', and she'd fantasised about a life at St Martin's College, hanging out with pale folk who pretended that they were French. 'Jarv' had also unveiled a new song called 'Disco 2000', and she'd wondered what she would be doing at this time, five years on. The answer, of course, was that she'd be in the Healing Field, French-kissing Gemma in what would become a legendary three-day experiment with lesbianism.

To those who will listen, Lucy will moan about the new, 'tame' Glastonbury, fondly recalling the time she watched Ian Brown haircuts illegally streaming through a hole in the fence. Secretly, however, she quite likes it. She's always been lucky in Michael Eavis's kingdom, remaining untouched as those around her have had tents and wallets stolen and been felt up by itinerant weirdos. Now, with the new ID system and pricier tickets, the likelihood of crossing paths with drug dealers and deviants is smaller, so she can pass out happily in the Sacred Space after seven pints of cider, relatively free of worries. Sometimes she will emerge from her mini-coma to shout incoherently at Susie and Gemma, and it will be up to them to drag her back to the tents, wondering on the way why Lucy actively prohibits the use of the word 'tits!' in any other environment, but feels comfortable saying it four times an hour here for no logical reason. Later, when she sobers up slightly and hears some suspicious noises coming from the tent next door, she will say, a little louder than is called for, 'Are those two *shagging*?' The next morning, she will be bright and breezy, bubbly about the prospect of seeing Jools Holland, the Backbeat Beatles, Brian Wilson and 17 other acts she would normally rather sell her old Adidas school trainers than admit to liking. As the three girls pass by the exact patch of ground where Lucy once split up with one of her boyfriends because he didn't like the Cure, Gemma stares at her friend and tries to see the clerical worker beneath the pigtails. 'But I thought you hated the Beach Boys, Luce,' she says. Lucy looks back, bewildered, and adjusts the droopy fluorescent novelty hat she brought the previous day. 'Yeah, but Gem – it's Glasters, isn't it?'

THE SPONGE

Daniel knows that, in the cut and thrust of night life,
what matters is the odd well-chosen nugget of knowledge.

'ME? I'M TOTALLY into the seventies – *totally*,' says Daniel,
clapping his hands and clicking his fingers in a hyperactive way that
suggests that, at any moment, he could start re-enacting a move
from *Saturday Night Fever*, right here, in the middle of the
microbrewery. Linda, who has travelled from Blackburn to
Newcastle for her friend's hen night but temporarily lost the rest of
the party, is amused. 'Isn't that a bit odd,' she thinks, 'viewing a
decade as if it were a genre?' But it's just a brief thought – there is
rarely time for anything more, when a schizophrenic verbal

whirlwind like Dan is around – and not one she has time to compute fully before he is leading her back to the dance floor by the elbow. She'd assumed at first that he was a typical nocturnal Casanova – perhaps it was the damp-looking Hoxton fin and the foamy smile – but you have to give it to this guy: he seems to know his stuff. 'Have you ever heard "Machine Gun" by the Commodores?' he barks into her ear. 'Now – I'm telling you; that is a fuckin' tuuuuune. Much more down and dirty than their later stuff. Hard to believe it's the same band who did "Three Times a Lady".'

Were passion measured by possessions alone, Daniel might be viewed as someone for whom music has little significance. As he will proudly tell those closest to him, he still owns only three CDs: *The Best of Seal*, *Now … That's What I Call Music 15* and Coldplay's *X and Y* (this last being something of a white lie, since it was burned off his mate Jerry's computer). Despite his claim to be on the verge of investing in an MP3 player for almost three years, his disposable income continues to go on more transient pleasures, many of which will have ceased to take corporeal form by the time the cold light of morning rolls around.

He knows that, in the cut and thrust of night life, it doesn't matter how many Neil Young biographies you own: what matters is the odd well-chosen nugget of knowledge. Combine this with a confidently held gaze, a good ear, a promising smile and a couple of nifty moves, and you're laughing.

Quieter, more serious friends thrash pop trivia back and forth in the pub while Daniel slips into a virtual coma of apparent boredom, then watch, stunned, an hour later in the club as Dan neatly deploys edited highlights of their conversation to help ensnare his prey – whether that prey be another brief, thrilling romantic conquest, or another culturally learned pal to bounce off.

'Of course, Frank Zappa said that most rock journalism is people who can't write interviewing people who can't talk for people who can't read,' he will say, as his hand slips down onto the buttock of the shapely student-newspaper editor with the nose ring and the White Stripes T-shirt.

The next night, at the happy-house place near the Bigg Market with a different group of friends, he'll be no less at home. The only musical genre he has ever struggled to paste himself to is folk, but that wasn't for lack of trying. 'Sure – I love that shit. The protest stuff is my favourite,' he told the girl with the endless hair and the peasant blouse whom Jonesy, a club promoter mate, introduced him to. 'The Corrs, Shakespeare's Sister. Fuckin' class. I even went to the Cropredy festival the other year. Saw that band the dead woman used to be in. Fairport Attraction.'

Nobody would ever question Daniel's passion for music – seeing him lifted out of the trudge of his nondescript marketing job with Capital One by the magic of the dance floor can't fail to lift the spirits of anyone who knows him – but people sometimes wonder what really gets under his skin, what really touches him, what drives him up the wall. Sometimes it's unnerving, watching someone show equal happy-go-lucky enthusiasm for the latest And You Will Know Us By the Trail of Dead album and *The Best of Peter Kay* in the space of ten minutes. He will always be the one man in a group of close friends who is reluctant to answer the question, 'What song would you want played at your funeral?'

His enthusiasm for music is always just enough to take him successfully through the night and not much further, and is a perfect fit for his slightly distracted, higher-than-average sex drive. Similarly, his clothing betrays an easily sidetracked, malleable mind – a mixture of too-tight paisley shirts, quick-drying manmade fibres, shiny sporting apparel, needlessly intricate trainers, bandannas and ill-advised, graffiti-strewn jackets intended for part-formed males 10 years his junior. But, for a man with a low boredom threshold, he makes some odd decisions. Just recently, he was in Waterstone's with his mature-student friend, Pete, and found himself paying for a copy of *You Bright and Risen Angels* by William T. Vollmann.

Because the last time Pete had seen Daniel ensconced in any book besides Schott's *Original Miscellany* was a decade and a half ago, during A-level English, Pete thought it a bit strange that his friend would choose to ease himself into a zeal for literature with a 600-page-plus treatise on a future world where humanoid insects do battle with the inventors of electricity.

A couple of weeks later, in the pub, he enquired how Dan was progressing with Vollman's semicolon-heavy style. The answer was garbled, however, and, before Pete knew it, Kajagoogoo's 'Too Shy' was on the jukebox and Dan was making a beeline across the room towards a blonde girl in deelyboppers he was almost certain he may or may not have met at Tyneside Cinema the previous Christmas. 'The eighties,' Pete watched his friend say, as he brushed the dry-roasted peanut crumbs off his Adidas tracksuit top. 'Now – you can't tell me that that wasn't a time when music was real.'

THE REFORMED ROCKER

*Back in the day, on the Mosely scene,
Paulette was known as 'Satan's Kitten'.*

'WHAT'S THAT TUNE?' thinks Paulette, for the umpteenth time since she got out of bed this morning. She hates that – when it's right there, going around your head, but the name is just out of reach, teasing you, donkey-and-carrot style. Wiping a globule of jam from the top of the gear stick – a sign that Nathan was using it as a pretend joystick again while she nipped into the post office – she thinks hard, shutting out the early-morning fury of the M6. She can see everything but the name in her head. Possibly late Judas Priest? Maybe one of Ronnie James Dio's more intense moments? Then it hits her: 'Do the Lollipop' by the Tweenies. That's it! She might have known.

This happens a lot to Paulette these days. She'll be sauntering along the corridor, on the way to meet with an architect or a contractor, and suddenly she'll find herself humming the theme from Balamory or a song from the Bob the Builder CD. This isn't a matter of choice: it is humanly impossible to hear 'Let's Get Busy' 78 times a week without its snaking its way into your subconscious. Perhaps most frightening of all was the time she was having a fag break, idly staring out towards the new Selfridges building, and her assistant, Sharon, asked her what it was that she kept whistling. Paulette hadn't even realised she'd been making a sound, but she'd thought for a moment and realised that the tune was the one she and Steve had made up for Halford's potty time ('poo poo poo / poo poo poo / do a little poo poo poo / it … goes … plop!'). She was just glad it had been whistling she'd been doing, not singing.

Paulette knows her mates think she's sold out. She and Steve prefer to think of it as 'selling in' – anything she's done in the last five years to make money has been purely for the benefit of Halford, Nathan and Steve. And, besides, she's still got the leather pants – sometimes even wears them for country walks at weekends – and Steve's still got his bikes and mane of black hair. She said she'd never get tied down, of course, but that was before Steve showed her a kind of commitment that she'd never suspected men of 18 stone with beards and Kawasakis were capable of. What? Did Kaz, Dosser and Charlotte think she was still going to be down on the front row at Donington, watching Maiden, trying to get Bruce Dickinson to smile at her, after Halford arrived and they converted the first water mill and got lucky? There's no let-up in property development: you have to keep on pushing. She's sure the girls are happy for her, but sometimes, when Kaz sends her a lengthy email about, for example, seeing Cold Chisel in Australia, she'll feel a prickle of envy. In return, she'll wind her up by sending a reply consisting solely of eight baby photographs, titled 'Halford In His Nappy'. Her head fogged with Fimbles, it will escape Paulette's notice (but not Kaz's) that an email with the same heading in the subject box, sent in the past, might easily have consisted of rather more licentious content, relating to a well-known metal singer. You never knew with Paulette, back in the day, when, on the Mosely scene, she was known as 'Satan's Kitten'.

A couple of years ago, Kaz bought Paulette a CD called *Rock Baby* to play to Halford, featuring, among others, lullaby versions of 'She Sells Sanctuary', 'Smoke on the Water' and 'The Boys Are Back in Town'. Paulette and Steve loved the concept, but they generally find that their taste runs more to 'Nellie the Elephant'. Kaz found it difficult to hide her horror a couple of weeks later when she visited them at the new barn conversion in Shifnal and saw *Rock Baby* out of its case, scratched and stuffed under a pile of Mr Men tea coasters – a horror that was compounded when, later in the evening, as Halford and Nathan's bedtime approached, Steve and Paulette started to refer to each other as 'Mrs Mummy' and 'Mr Daddy'. Four days later, Kaz forced Paulette to come out and see the Banger Sisters at the Odeon. Just for a moment, in the pub afterwards, the old Paulette was evident, but, by the time they'd got back in Kaz's Ford Capri, she could see that her mind had turned back to the responsible world, just by the way she was fiddling with her Boobah key-ring. Now, she's trying to get her to listen to this band, the Darkness. She knows she should have heard them by now and that their first album sold loads. Apparently, the guitarist is really skinny and hot, but, as Kaz should know by now, Paulette likes her men more on the cuddly side.

THE REGGAE POSER

*Della doesn't shop at supermarkets,
unless they are foreign and family-run.*

'DO YOU WANT any coffee?' asks Della, adopting that special tone of reverence that she seems to use only in the arena of hot drinks. 'It's, like, Brazilian and shit – from the market.' She's entertaining again, and the sound of Toots and the Maytals' 'Pressure Drop' skanks away in the living room, niggling at her flatmate, Rod, who, having graduated in creative writing a year late, is working furiously on his telemarketing-themed play, *Eye of the Tiger*. 'Don't worry about him,' she tells Marcel, her second gentleman companion of the week, as she sashays through the love beads in the doorway, before silently mouthing the word 'philistine'.

Della sees Rod in much the same way as she sees a good 98 per cent of the population: not as someone who's made his own choice about his musical preference and decided that the likes of Bob Marley, Toots and Eekamouse don't really do it for him, but as someone who was simply never fortunate enough to be converted to reggae. She played the benefactor for a while, of course, invited him down to the roots night some hip folk at the Corn Exchange turned her on to, but he always seemed to find an excuse. Then, after he seemed thoroughly unimpressed by the Haile Selassie poster she put up in the living room, she started to ignore him, talking to him only when it looked as if they were out of toilet roll or sugar. Della often finds herself short on the essentials of day-to-day living, since she doesn't shop at supermarkets, unless they are foreign and family-run. 'A Heavy Atmosphere Centre of Corporo Hate', she called the central Cambridge branch of Sainsbury's not long ago, when forced to visit it with her mum, who was short on fabric conditioner.

At the weekend, she hits the markets and stocks up on products that require paper bags. These places are full of tourists, of course, this being Cambridge, but she can live with that, since she knows, deep down, she stands out, and not just because of her multicoloured armbands, dreadlocks and Nordic good looks. As she buys her pulses, she talks earnestly about their origins to the stallholders, nodding copiously, sometimes even going so far as to squat by their side, froglike, should the conversation get deep. Later, she might pick up a new djenbe drum, which she will never play.

Della's mum, Annika, is Swedish and moved over to the UK in the seventies. Della has never met her dad, who disappeared before she was born, or even seen a photo of him, for that matter, but she pictures him as culturally open, like herself: not so much a fly-by-night chancer as a cultural mop who just had to keep absorbing and couldn't be pinned down. Her basis for this image is one somewhat scratchy Big Youth album, featuring a man with dreadlocks engulfed by a cloud of dope, and a copy of the *Karma Sutra*: the sole items her mum inherited from him, both of which now reside in Della's bedroom. Annika hasn't the heart to tell her he was a roofing contractor who holidayed in Majorca.

Every Friday at seven, she joins some other people in well-insulated hats in the local community hall, for a class in Capuera, which she describes to friends as 'the martial art that's beyond contact'. Here, she gets the chance to vent the frustration that has built up during the course of the week without actually beating anyone up. She feels chilled and wholesome afterwards, ready to kick back with Jackie Mittoo and Marcel, have a little Tantric sex, and possibly think about the plight of the oppressed.

'You like this?' she asks him, as a new Toots song begins, and she lowers herself onto his lap. 'This speaks to me. You know wot I'm saying, man?'

He nods with her, thinking this is possibly not the best time to admit his favourite song in the genre is 'Uptown Top Ranking' by Althea and Donna. He goes to kiss her, but she springs off him and reaches for a Rizla, which she rolls, lights and smokes with exaggeratedly cupped hands. Then she moves over to open the sash windows, wide. It's time, once more, to spread the word.

THE ONE-MAN WOMAN

Christine is glad that Cliff lets her know about his albums and tours through his website. A lot of other artists wouldn't go to the bother.

CHRISTINE SIGHS, WIPES the excess water meticulously from the top of her hot-water bottle and happily resigns herself to another date with the only man who cares. She dabs her pulse points with another drop of Miss You Nights, opens a new box of Terry's All Gold, gets out her special, silver, stork-shaped sewing scissors and leafs through this week's edition of *Let's Talk!* magazine. Surely there will be a clipping for her scrapbook this time around. It's been almost four weeks! She turns on the stereo – a 1991 Madzuwisha midi system she inherited from her daughter, Samantha – keeping it at a gentle volume, not noticing the technology's way of making even the most cleanly mastered CD sound as though it were being broadcast through an item of thermal underwear. Meanwhile, her Westie terrier, Bachelor Boy, snores happily at her feet on his embroidered 'Joy To All Our Friends' cushion.

Christine is married to Derek, a deputy manager of an office-supplies company, and he discourages her from attending his regular meet-and-greets. He's trying to keep his head above water in an office full of people 30 years younger than he is, and it's not easy when all your wife will talk about is Cliff Richard. 'But you're only forty-eight for chrissakes!' he will plead. 'Grant's wife is older than you and she was talking to the MD about that rapper man, Fifty Pence or whatever he's called; you just kept making him smell your Cliff Richard perfume!' '*Sir* Cliff,' she corrects him, but he's out of the door. Samantha has hidden herself away upstairs somewhere. If only they were all as loyal as Bachelor Boy.

She wonders whether she might be able to find something on the Internet – a snatch of news, a photo, at the very least. She considers herself fairly adept with modern technology, but this Google thing Samantha has been telling her about is a worry. What about those hackers? Can't they see what you're searching for? She's glad that Cliff is so kind, letting her know about his albums and tours through his website. A lot of other artists wouldn't go to the bother. She just wishes the updates were a bit more frequent – especially now that, following the distressing business with the council and the woman next door with her *very* unchristian attitude, she no longer feels comfortable listening to his actual records as often or as loudly as she'd like to.

She knows it's not Cliff's fault that he's more low-profile than he used to be. He'd never deny his fans. It's probably all those radio station controllers and trendy music-business people who think he's too old. Too old! What a joke that is! They didn't say that about that Pete Entwistle bloke, before all those drugs took their toll and he died with that prostitute. She knows Cliff will outlast them all. The fact is, though, she needs more. She longs for the glory days of the chat show, when she'd sit in the chair next to the mock-Tudor TV cabinet, the video permanently set to 'pause-record' in case he would appear. If it wasn't a guest slot on *Wogan*, sandwiched between Les Dennis and Joan Collins, then it would be a celebrity fun run or, at the very least, Wimbledon. Christine nearly choked on her Findus Crispy Pancake that time it rained and he led the Centre Court crowd in a singalong. What would she have done to be Virginia Wade that day! For the next three years she queued for match tickets on days when the forecast was for showers, but never got lucky.

Now that the twice-weekly additions to the clippings and video library – each tape stored safely in a plastic case shaped like an antique book – have dwindled, she wonders whether attending church more often would bring her closer to Cliff. There is also always the option of a club night she read about in her *Daily Mail* called Guilty Pleasures, where they play 'Devil Woman' and 'Wired for Sound', but in her humble opinion the other songs quoted as being on the playlist sounded a little bit old and cheesy. She thinks back to when she last danced. It must have been 1999, when Cliff played Hyde Park. What a day that was! It truly had it all. Culture (that sweet boy, Russell Watson, whom Cliff invited on stage, and who sang 'Nessun Dorma' so beautifully). Sex appeal (that Billy Idol bloke might think he invented punk, but has he ever heard 'Move It'?). Elaine Page (very pleasant, although there is an age when a woman should realise that a certain kind of footwear is no longer dignified). And then that snotty man from the *Guardian* – the one who compared the atmosphere to a bowling match – whom Christine wrote to and gave a piece of her mind. She considers her sign-off – 'Now, as you suggest, I'm going to put on my slippers and sip some Horlicks, and get tucked up in bed – it is almost nine pm, after all!' – one of the most witty of three decades of opinionated letter writing.

Actually, that gives her an idea! It must be two weeks since her last missive – a letter to the local branch of Somerfield to suggest that the kiosk tills be limited to 10 items or fewer – and she suddenly feels in a quarrelsome mood. Turning the stereo off – as she always does when she's not in the room with it, even if she's just nipped to the toilet or to boil the kettle – she goes into the kitchen, followed by Bachelor Boy, who stays a little less close to her heel than he would if she weren't wearing her strangely air-freshener-like talcum powder. She picks up her plain A5 pad with its single, accompanying lined sheet, and her veteran fountain pen, and is just considering who the recipient of tonight's complaint will be – the controller of Radio 3? Mr Fellows, the grumpy florist from down the road? – when she spots Derek's laptop on the work surface. Checking around for who knows who, she sheepishly opens it and finds Derek has already left a webpage open on the screen. Something about 'global auctions'. Seeing a button that says 'search', on an impulse Christine types her idol's name in the gap below. Shortly afterwards, her eyes widen. She wonders if Derek has taken his company credit card with him tonight.

THE POSH HIPPIE

The truth is, Nigel never really enjoyed himself in the sixties.

'NIGEL!' SHOUTS HERMIONE. 'The Portwell-Spencers are arriving at eleven and you still haven't put their organic poppy-seed wholemeal loaf out.' He can't hear her because the door's shut and the previously unreleased demo version of Buffalo Springfield's 'Hung Upside Down' is on. She'll see him again in two or three hours when he takes his afternoon swim. At least he made an attempt to start his chores this time – she can see that, from the plastic dustpan and brush left precariously on the hob of the cooker in Cottage Three. His easily distracted nature is sort of lovable, and boys have got to have their toys, she thinks. It could be worse:

Robert, the solicitor who's married to her friend Sally from the village, is 56 and he has a Scalextric.

'But isn't it a bit odd, having a Music Room?' she sometimes wonders. When Nigel initially suggested the idea, she'd assumed it would be an area for guests, or at least a place where there would be instruments for her and Nigel, and their families, to play. She hadn't for a moment imagined that it would be a soulless space, filled with nothing but vinyl, CDs and a stereo. What on earth would you do in there, after you'd put an album on, apart from fondling other albums? For her, music must always be accompanied by another activity – driving, cooking, scanning the latest issue of *Country Living*. She would never admit this, but it gives her the creeps to think of her husband up there, staring at his amplifier, as if, by the sheer act of focusing his attention on it, he could elicit more enjoyment from his copy of *Electric Ladyland*. The room is to her what the cupboard where her father kept his copies of *Playboy* was to her mother, and it's the one area of the house where the job of vacuuming falls to Nigel.

Nigel's life has been filled with psychedelic rock since his late teens. 'You can't change me, babe,' he said, when Hermione first met him at a blues club in Torquay, 15 years ago. It wasn't the first or last time he would use mock hippiespeak to disguise as a joke something he meant seriously. The constant loud volume isn't a problem out of season, since the nearest neighbours are two fields away, but when summer comes, and Nigel and Hermione rent out the cottages abutting their Georgian farmhouse, she has to explain that not everyone likes waking up to 'Sunshine of Your Love'. He'll sulk for a while, then swan out into the courtyard later that day, holding a glass of 1979 claret in a slightly camp manner. Before long, he'll be regaling the guests with the story of how he once pissed next to one of John Mayall's Bluesbreakers.

Nigel was actually something of an armchair hippie back in the late sixties and early seventies. He was at the Isle of Wight festival, but came home early after catching a cold and finding someone's puke in his shoe. At university, others in his hall of residence were always quicker to buy the latest hip albums. Later, desperate for dope and party money, they'd sell them on to Nigel, whom they'd never quite been able to take seriously since they saw him unpack a pestle and mortar from his parents' car at the start of term. From here, the roots of his LP collection spread and spread, until, finally, after much deliberation, he decided to replace it with CDs. Last month, he traded in his original copy of the Rotary Connection's *Dinner Music* for the CD reissue and came out £1.50 up on the deal. He went home happy, blissfully unaware that the dealer he sold the vinyl to would sell it on eBay 10 days later for over a hundred quid.

When Nigel arrives in Virgin Megastore in Exeter, the staff let out an involuntary shiver. It doesn't matter how many times they explain that it's against company policy to play CDs for customers, he doesn't seem to get it. He even started to irritate Matt, the twentysomething Crosby, Stills and Nash-loving sales assistant with the sideburns and the easygoing demeanour, after a while. For younger people who are interested in the legends of the sixties, Nigel can initially seem like a mine of spellbinding information, but the puritanical nature of his regurgitated facts, his evangelical belief in any highfalutin cultural event that took place between 1965 and 1974, can grate. Not that he'd imagine that he's boring anyone – he's enjoying himself too much. There have been fashion mistakes in the past – one thinks in particular of the 1990–2 period, when he enjoyed the status of Poshest Man In South Devon To Combine A Stetson With A Ponytail. But these days, aided by his baggy cords, cowboy shirts and chin stubble, he feels good in his own skin. He's read the biographies, seen the films, memorised the legends: his era feels special now – 'like the Renaissance in flares,' he once mused to himself. He feels ensconced in it in a way he never did back in the day. Truth is, he never really enjoyed himself in the sixties. But does anybody need to know that? Of course not – and they probably never will, since most of his friends from that era have long since lost touch. At a party thrown by Hermione last Wednesday he announced to a packed, impressed living room that he had been instrumental in the organisation of the Fourteen-Hour Technicolor Dream event at Alexander Palace in 1967. The frightening thing was: for a moment, even he believed himself.

THE HARD HOUSE HEADCASE

When Damian is in the booth, he feels 'like being in charge of a massive car, with two wheels and a shitload of passengers'.

'YOU HAVE NO idea what I feel when the music surges through me, so don't even try to judge me,' the 26-year-old Damian says to his mum. It's the same old argument: she says he should get himself a proper job and a flat of his own. He says deejaying is a proper job, and, if she wanted him to co-operate, she should have thought a bit more carefully about what she was doing back in 1991, when she left his dad for Ian, the postman with the pornographic snake tattoo on his back. He knows all the guilt tricks and he knows that, as long as she thinks his music is all he has to boost his self-esteem, she'll never be able to kick him out. On Friday nights, she and Ian retreat to the pub, leaving it all behind for a few hours, including the sympathetic stares of her neighbours: good, gentle retired folk, tired of watching their woodburner shake to a *Cut Your Own Samples* CD that came free with *Mixmag*. 'What does it mean now, this term, "DJ"?' the more sprightly minded of them wonder. Surely, however vague the term may be, it should mean Damian's out of the house in the evenings a bit more than this.

In truth, Damian's been a paid decks spinner three times thus far in his life. Once at Jimmy Snoozes in York (for three beers), once at a warehouse he can't remember getting to or leaving (for 20 quid) and once at the birthday part of his mate, Schnoz (for an E and the hell of it). It's not the most extensive CV, but all his heroes had to put in their time as apprentices too: Andy Farley, Judge Jules, the Tidy Boys, Scuzz the Communal Baboon. He sees himself as 'networking' at the moment – putting himself in the right place at the right time. Mostly, this will involve hanging around the decks in York's Cyberdog record shop, pulling faces that suggest the unravelling of a complicated mathematical equation, and using the phrase 'That's gravy' three times every ten minutes. After a nasty incident on the stairs at home with some maracas, Ian the Postman – a gentle fellow, despite the snake – has learned to stay out of Damian's way, but one time he couldn't help sneaking into Cyberdog to see where his stepson spends much of his daytime hours. What initially hit him, along with the vast amount of plastic and UV lighting, was the lack of records on display. After a short time listening to some people who looked like Damian but with slightly less close-set eyes talk about 'Fat Vegetable' – a club? a band? a record? – he staggered out onto the pavement, so dizzy he almost had to steady himself against a *Big Issue* seller.

Ian doesn't understand Damian and doesn't want to, any more than he wants to know the mystery behind Damian's permanently damp-looking middle-parted hair. Damian knows, deep down somewhere where he keeps the things he would never voice, that Ian probably thinks he's a manic depressive. But what does he know? He's just a boring old uptight fart who talks about nothing but bills and probably couldn't tell the difference between hooligan house and boompty boomp. If he ever saw Damian in his element, he'd know. They all would.

There's nothing quite like the way Damian feels when he's in the booth. 'Like being in charge of a massive car, with two wheels and shitloads of passengers,' he thought to himself in a moment of clarity, between rounds of *Grand Theft Auto* on his amped-up Xbox. It's not just the drugs that make it great. He loves the way strangers come up to him and pat him on the back when he plays a rinsing tune. The last time, at Daz's place, one guy even rapped to him. He couldn't make out much of what the bloke, who was dressed in a boiler suit with bits of toast stuck to it and introduced himself as Bongo, was saying, apart from 'bass in your face, one-two-three, everyone got tha bass', but it was an amazing moment. Creative, y'know? Spiritual. Later, copying another of his heroes, David Morales, Damian upped the mood by taking his T-shirt off. He looked out towards the sea of pumping hands – as many as 28 of them, in all – and experienced a feeling of control like nothing else in the world. It was eight months ago now, yet sometimes, when he closes his eyes in his room and turns his 'Funky Drummer' loop up to drown out the sound of his mum's tumble dryer, he can still taste it.

THE EURO ROCKERS

For Edgar and Annika, if it has a guitar, is loud and it makes you
want to punch the air, it's worth trekking around Europe for.

YOU KEEP YOUR head down while you wait for the tube and you
keep yourself to yourself, but Edgar, despite being a regular visitor
to London, hasn't yet quite worked this out. 'Chain, chain, chain!'
he sings to his girlfriend, Annika, loudly, pushing his face right up
into hers. 'Chain so coooooool!' She knows he's got the words
wrong, and that the other passengers on the platform are
exchanging nervously amused glances, but she would never point
this out. She's having too much fun. What would be the point of
trying to crush his spirit, just to pander to the jaded mores of people
with far less spirit than he has? Besides, he'd only move on to

another one of his greatest hits – 'Livin' on a Prayer', perhaps ('Take my hand and we'll make it elsewhere!') or 'I Am the Walrus' ('I am the head man /I am the Walrus!').

'Rock' is a big, much-encompassing term, but Edgar and Annika are big people with big hair who can happily mosh around in every aspect of it. For them, there are no subgenres, no dividing line of cool that separates Bon Jovi from the Beatles, nothing to separate *Shake Your Money Maker* from 'Shakermaker'. Quite simply, if it has a guitar, is loud and makes you want to punch the air, it's worth shouting about and trekking around Europe for.

When a camera pans through a crowd in the front row of a festival, Annika and Edgar are the people pulling the silly snarling faces and doing horns signs at the lens. A typical summer for them will take in around fifty gigs, leaving few weekends free for the other activities they relish, such as paintballing, parachuting and rewatching Burt Reynolds movies. For the purposes of their adventures, they will rarely stray from cultural uniforms that encapsulate their lack of discrimination between the last four decades: a bright PVC bomber jacket, torn denim, bangles and heels for Annika, a skin-tight Led Zeppelin T-shirt, drainpipe jeans and baseball boots for Edgar. Alone, their colour schemes might clash, but, when they stand next to one another, they make a strange kind of sense. While on the road, they will compile a scrapbook of their experiences, which will include various reunion-tour ticket stubs, a photograph of one of Uriah Heep biting Edgar's nose, a set list from a show by the Australian Doors, and a picture of Annika looking disappointed outside the former site of the Rock Circus waxwork museum in Piccadilly Circus. Despite sleeping between itchy bed sheets in damp rooms with thin walls and spending much of their time in crowded places, they will both remain Zen and unruffled. If anyone gets on their nerves, they will usually laugh it off and use their favourite put-down: 'Joker!'

Typically, the summer will end with Alice Cooper looking into the front row and singing 'Only Women Bleed' to Annika (again), or – if Alice isn't on the reunion trail this year – a visit to Jim Morrison's tombstone at Père Lachaise. At this point, Edgar will show his first sign of melancholy for three months, go a bit poetic, and nonchalantly destroy some roadworks on the way back to the hotel. Then it will be back home to Rotterdam, where both of them will continue to study for their degrees in astrophysics, and Edgar will continue to neglect to replace the cracked windscreen on his 1986 Ford Escort, drive too fast, and listen to a DJ shout 'Rock temple!' for the hell of it on Holland's most-listened-to oldies station. Annika will do some part-time work in a local karaoke bar and Edgar will supplement his grant by selling autographs on eBay and emailing bemused strangers in Australia about the time that Slash gave him a personal lesson in air guitar ('He really did it, man – can you believe what a rocking living-on-the-edge dude that cat is?'). By spending their nights only in the pubs with a high quota of leather jackets and 'Bat Out of Hell' on the jukebox, they will never be forced to reject drum'n'bass or grime or hip-hop. These genres simply won't penetrate their universe. Just occasionally, they will get the inkling that there is another musical belief system out there, where Supertramp and Steve Miller are not considered fashionable, but, as quickly as they register its existence, they will dismiss it. If they encounter someone who seems to think he or she is better than they, cooler than they, they tend to use their own little code. 'Some people call me the Space Cowboy / Some call me the counsellor of love!' Edgar will sing, and Annika will know immediately what it means – that they're dealing with a Joker, a non-believer; someone outside the Bubble of Rock, who could never understand.

SENSITIVE WORLD MUSIC GUY

You can slag off Edward's sensible tweed jackets all you like.
Dis his Diblo Dibala, though, and he'll see red.

THERE ARE A lot of things that wind Edward up. Ringtones, builders, Robert Kilroy Silk, taxi drivers, being called 'Eddie'. Mostly, he is able to retain a calm, open-minded demeanour – the demeanour of a 1992 issue of *Q* magazine, the demeanour of a late Peter Gabriel album – in the face of all this. One way *really* to get at him, however, is to insult his music. You can slag off his sensible tweed jackets all you like. You can mock his strict adherence to the speed limit, guffaw at the way he pinches the gear stick between his forefinger and thumb like a tender lover. He'll just smile. Dis his Diblo Dibala, though, and he'll see red. If he's really mad, he might even drive off for a sulk in his Toyota Prius for periods of up to two hours. Just him, an early Franco and L'OK Jazz album, and the open road.

His art student son, Ben, learned about 'Red Ed' the hard way. He'd really just been having a laugh when he said that, with English lyrics, Ali Farka Toure's Niafunke would 'just be schmaltzy, mainstream crap'. He certainly didn't expect Edward to slam the greenhouse door so hard it smashed a pain of glass – not Edward, with his peaceful brogues and his collection of conga drums. A couple of days later, when his dad was still barely speaking to him and refused to give him a lift to the local independent cinema, he knew he'd really touched a nerve, soiled something spiritual.

Edward is one of those fiftysomething men who think of their early middle age, not their youth, as their halcyon days. Not for him the musical milestones of most of his generation. Dusty Springfield? Eric Clapton? Facile pretenders who stole the black men's music and watered it down. What he looks back on with real fondness is the days when Andy Kershaw had a prime-time slot on Radio 1, the days of Paul Simon's rhythmical rebirth, the days when getting an editing job at *Folk Roots* magazine didn't seem like the far-off dream of a younger liberal. He's a tall man, with a sensitively stooping posture who, when not getting muddled up with the voicemail function on his mobile phone, can often be found in his office at the north-eastern English university, where he works, sitting with his hands on his knees talking in an exaggeratedly smooth, quiet voice to his Scriptwriting for Stage students. 'This really speaks to me,' he will tell the most promising ones, handling their essays – which is exactly what he said the first time he heard the Bhundu Boys. In those days, he called what he listened to 'world music'. He shudders at the term now. These days, it's just 'music'.

While Edward's wife, Jane, would never describe herself as an authority on African pop, she gets caught up in the slipstream of Edward's enthusiasm, and can get a little bit carried away dancing around the living room to it after a couple too many glasses of the red wine they brought back from last year's holiday in the Massif Central. Similarly, her conscientious clean living is something he supports, without being a full-time spokesperson for it. On trips as a visiting lecturer, he has been known to make a clandestine stop at Burger King (only for a spicy beanburger, mind). Truth be told, if he wasn't with Jane, he'd probably drive a Saab, not a Prius. She, meanwhile, spends as much time on the bicycle as possible, and can be heard to shout her own special brand of polite insult when cut up by motorists on Durham's one-way system ('I'm doing my bit for the environment; how about you?'). It amazes Edward that they (he supposes they can be described as old folks now, but they don't feel it) are the ones listening to the music with the real energy – so different from those sulky, static rock bands that Ben watches on MTV 2.

Jane won't come to London with him, because of the pollution, and, when he's browsing through the Zaïrean section of Sterns record shop, he feels a unique kind of freedom. Sometimes, he can spend hours in there, sampling the stock, and networking with other, equally softly spoken men, many of whom have, at an earlier, less balanced point in their lives, toyed with the idea of wearing an ear stud. He wonders what would have happened if he'd moved to London when he was young. Would he have played pedal steel for a living? Would he now attend parties at the house of Richard Thompson, and not at the house of an earthy couple who go to the toilet on a bed of reeds and give homemade soap as Christmas presents? It's not in his nature to dwell on what might have been, but these things prey on his mind briefly, as he drives up the M1. By the time he's bypassing Doncaster, though, he's lost in the rhythms of a new French hip-hop CD and, once again, he feels happy with his lot. Sweeping Ben's Kaiser Chiefs album off the passenger seat onto the floor, he turns the volume up, and performs a swift dancing lunge, his leg catching the clutch and making the engine rev slightly. 'Being relevant,' he thinks to himself, 'is just a state of mind.'

THE ETERNAL STUDENT

*It never occurs to Karen that there's anything strange
about having taste that froze in the early nineties.*

FIVE MONTHS AGO, Karen's marriage finally disintegrated.
Leaving her computer technician husband Charlie was surprisingly
straightforward in the end: she just loaded up the Peugeot 205, said
goodbye to the Japanese fighting fish and headed for the flat rented
by Derek, her friend from her herbalism evening class. She's been
there ever since, and, if she overlooks the time-worn poster of a half-
naked Anna Friel on the living room wall, can easily convince
herself it's one of the happiest periods of her life. In retrospect, she
feels she did 'the whole getting-hitched thing' too young, though she
felt ancient enough at the time, in her final year at Bristol University
– 1991, or was it 1992? Her last memory of free single life is seeing
James play at Alton Towers. Now, she's turning into a Friends

Reunited junkie, hooking up with the people she knew back then, and she liked to think she knew everyone. 'What have you been up to for all this time?' they ask her, and she's always stumped to think of anything significant. Never mind: she's making up for lost time with Derek and the gang from Slater Deane Systems, living it up and spinning the old favourites: Inspiral Carpets, Northside, the Farm. It never occurs to her that there's anything strange about having taste that froze in the early nineties.

She doesn't see herself staying in telesales – or 'marketing', as they called it at the interview – but at the moment she's still grateful to Derek just for getting her the job, though not quite grateful enough to submit to his drunken requests for a snog. It struck her the other day that, if you discount a paper round when she was fourteen, she's never been employed before. Perhaps this is why she never seems to have any paper money on her and has a reputation for wheedling her way out of taxi fares. After the pub on Friday, it's all back to Derek's, though now the parties are strictly confined to the flat, which has an aroma that people mistake for marijuana (it's actually some hemp-flavoured joss that Karen's had since before River Phoenix died). At the end of the summer, the young couple in the flat below were kind enough to allow Karen and Derek to have a 'barbecue' in their garden, but things got out of hand, with a number of disturbing events taking place outside the couple's bedroom window between 3 and 5 am, including a pair of temps dry-humping and a union representative getting carried away on some bongos to 'Riders on the Storm'.

Karen's voice changes at these parties from a slightly gravelly off-kilter rumble to something that once prompted a bystander at the 1989 Reading Festival to enquire, 'Who's that fucking fishwife?' Drunk not only on cider but on the knowledge that she was there, at the hub, during the original release of the Mock Turtles' 'Can U Dig It', she shrieks a lot, bounces around, stamps on the odd ankle with her Doc Martens, and enthuses with the remainder of the

Slater Deane lot about the high quota of creative types living in the Greater Bristol area. 'Did you know there's even a street where all those trip-hop musicians live next door to one another?' someone says. Karen nods, and wonders what trip-hop is. She imagines it's a bit like Jesus Jones, but with even more keyboards.

Do Karen's male workmates find her sexually attractive? Sort of, though her energy frightens them and her clothes are so baggy they can never be too sure what shape she is. One thing is for certain: she's the life and soul of the party. She may have been out of action for a few years, but her active university life – a great success in everything but her final grade, a 2.2 in sociology – gave her ample qualifications in the etiquette of living it up. Should there be a lull in proceedings at one of Derek's shindigs, she'll be straight to the centre of things, making everyone in the room sit down to James's 1991 hit, 'Sit Down', or sing along to Janis Joplin's 'Mercedes Benz': it never fails! Then, the next morning, she'll be the first downstairs, taking care of the carnage with her bright-yellow Dyson vacuum cleaner, her third favourite possession after her Dockers and her signed Mary Whitehouse Experience T-shirt. Soon, she plans to go travelling: she'll probably hit India first, read *Memoirs of a Geisha* on the way. There are the music festivals, too: she always laughs when she thinks of the time she fell on Charlie's tent at Reading, almost suffocating him. But her immediate objective is to get her workmates out to a club. After all, someone must still be playing the Charlatans' 'The Only One I Know' somewhere.

THE MINI MOGUL

*Jason's mum worries: is it normal for a 14-year-old
to check the progress of the FTSE this much?*

FOURTEEN IS A volatile age and nobody is more aware of that than Hattie. She has only to look at her own adolescence for ample evidence that a placid childhood is no guarantee of a lack of future fireworks. She supposes she came out of it nicely enough – anyone who owns their own law practice can say they've done reasonably well for themselves in life – but she now realises that hands-off parenting is a lot easier in theory than practice. She'd always felt she'd been blessed, having a quiet, studious son like Jason, but, as his adolescence came to fruition, she found herself worrying that he might lack the social skills that he would need to get into the top-notch university of her dreams. The advert in the local paper for the

Lottery-funded youth initiative couldn't have come at a better time.

If she was being honest, she would say that at the time she didn't really think a lot about what would come of sending Jason to Soundz Wickid. She supposed it might be a distraction, a shell opener – a socially active change from those slightly odd robot-building sessions that Jason indulged in with his C of E schoolfriend Henry and her son's other, more worrying after-school activities (was it normal for a 14-year-old to check the progress of the FTSE this much?). That, and she was impressed by the top-of-the-range recording equipment in the catalogue. For the first few days Jason was overwhelmed by the raucous enthusiasm and one-upmanship of his peers and spent most of his time examining the back of the digital mixing desk. He soon realised that he still wasn't going to morph into an extrovert around all these larger-than-life personalities, quite a few of whom he suspected had been directed to the scheme in a last ditch attempt to curb their mildly criminal behaviour. He could count the number of schoolfriends he saw out of school on the thumb of one hand, but most of the Soundz Wickid crowd seemed to have an enormous network of friends, connected by a constant flow of text messages with strange smiley faces and savage abbreviations. Nobody seemed to pay much attention to him that week, but all the time he was watching and listening – the possible retail mark-up cost on those strangely baggy, brightly coloured nylon garments made a deep impression on his fertile mind – and he did experience a mild subversive frisson to think that his mother was completely unaware that she had forced him to mingle with people who smoked.

Slowly, Jason began to blend in. After the first week he found that his peers didn't stare at him as much if he kept his head constantly bobbing as each one stepped up to the mike (he also noticed that calling it a 'microphone' wasn't helping his cause much, either). As various people disappeared for what seemed like endless fag breaks, he would stay behind and watch Bertie, the grizzled engineer and supervisor, work the console and ask pertinent questions. 'I thought he didn't stand a chance in hell with the Soundz Wickid bunch,' Bertie would tell journalists later, shortly after Jason was featured in *Newsweek's* 'Junior Entrepreneurs' feature. 'I was wayyy wrong on that one.'

It was when Killa Gripz, Soundz Wickid's resident rap crew, approached him for technical help, on the grounds that he was a 'massive Brainiac', that Jason found his true niche both at the studio and in the world at large. The Killas' lead MC, Kay-Gee, may not have had any difficulty constructing elaborate machine-gunned elegies on the themes of graffiti, trainers and other people's mothers, but he urgently required assistance with a tricky piece of HTML on his posse's Geocities site. Within days Jason had written them an entire, different, much-improved site, containing cutting-edge Flash animations and offering sample downloads of their best tracks. By the end of the week, everyone else at the studio was getting his or her music added to a slickly constructed directory, featuring a profile of each of the Soundz Wickid students. While uploading the tracks, he improved Bertie's mixes using a self-written program on the sly. With the enormous network of friends he'd spotted, the number of hits on the site allowed him to start selling advertising space.

After the site brought wider attention to the more accomplished performers, Jason was trusted enough to examine the odd rough contract that came their way, and he could explain in simple terms just how the four hidden clauses he'd located meant that a third of all foreseeable earnings would be heading to somebody else's offshore account. He got Henry in to make some low-budget, effects-heavy music videos to send to local cable stations, his little friend's fascination with the female anatomy making the finished item highly compelling to their teen audience. And, by last year, SoundzWickid.com had blossomed from a free web audition network to a pay-per-download music label, bringing in advertising fees of a quarter of a million a year (allowing Jason to pay his artists a much lower fee for representation). The events he organises to promote the label always sell out in days thanks to the site's enormous subscription list. People have to work very hard to get his attention.

None of this is quite what Hattie had bargained for, and she is slightly worried by the GET RICH OR DIE TRYIN' poster that adorns his bedroom wall. She's fearful that he won't want to go to university now; the idea of hearing any child of hers use the phrase 'school of life' chills her to the bone. He's still kind and respectful Jason, and she's happy to see that he's rejected the baggy jeans and sideways golf visor of her nightmares for a preppy combination of tailored cashmere and tweed with vintage brogues. Notorious BIG's caveat of 'Mo Money, Mo Problems' has yet to have any relevance to his life, and seems unlikely to at any foreseeable future time. Nonetheless, there are still pressing concerns. At breakfast Hattie watches him juggle a Blackberry and a Sidekick, negotiating new signings and selling advertising space while he munches happily on his Cheerios. He now has a car service pick him up for school, since this allows him an extra half-hour of deal making before assembly and prayers. What he hasn't told her is that her education worries are unfounded: he has already been accepted to do an MBA at Harvard. He thinks he'll take it, but reckons that, if he does, he'll probably commute, in order to stay at the centre of operations.

It is, like he explained to the rather perplexed admissions officer on the phone: he likes what they are putting on the table, but he has a few other deals in the pipeline, bubbling under.

THE CAREWORKER

Is Judy a publicist? Not quite. A promoter? No. A manager? Almost.

BLEARILY, MIGUEL REACHES for the phone, knocking his half-full can of Red Bull onto his original copy of Lester Bangs's *Psychotic Reactions and Carburettor Dung*. What he babbles into the mouthpiece is not a hello, but a leftover sentence from his dream – something about a group of go-go dancers who had agreed to do a residence at the club. The shrill New Jersey voice on the other end of the line seems unperturbed. 'Hi, Miguel? It's Judy here? Judy – with Doug Sipmeyer?' Sipmeyer. Where does he know that name? That's right: the singer-songwriter he has booked to play the club in a month or so – kind of washed up now, but a hellraiser in his day, one of the best from the punkier side of the late seventies country scene. But who is this he's speaking to? The name rings a bell, but he can't quite place it. A publicist? Not quite. A promoter? No. A manager? Almost. As he grabs around in the pickled recesses of his brain to find where he has heard her voice before, he looks at the clock: 3.17 am. 'I know it's early,' continues the voice. 'But Doug and I have a very heavy schedule over the next few days, and I know, what with the bombing, you have been worried, but I wanted to confirm to you that Doug will, despite the rumours, be making the trip to Barcelona. OK? We know you guys will be glad to hear that, and we don't want to let you down. OK? Good to speak to you! Have a fantastic day now.' With a mumble, Miguel replaces the phone back into the cradle, turns over, and farts. Before he returns to sleep, he has just one thought: 'What rumours?'

Back in Austin, Texas – her adopted home – Judy fingers her to-do list, and uses her ruler to neatly cross out job number 6, 'Tell Spanish venues that Doug will still be coming over'. Somewhere on her conscience is a vague notion that the call she has just made wasn't of the most sociable nature, but some things just have to be done at the earliest possible opportunity. Besides – these south European places are all 24-hour cities these days, aren't they? The truth is, she saw the report of the bombing in Oporto, and, even though it was only a small one, and just a couple of people were injured, and, yes, Oporto isn't *technically* in Spain, she knows how Europeans feel about the Americans' *sensitivity* when it comes to acts of terrorism, and she wanted to put any doubts to rest. 'Slipknot and Eminem might balk in the face of a plane crash, but not Sipmeyer! Not on your ass!' she thinks, as she closes down her husband's webpage for the night and rushes across the house to add a Nantucket-briar bath bomb to the Jacuzzi tub before the water overflows (she hopes that for once Doug remembers not actually to activate the jets, since the discharge from the bomb clogs them up).

Spain has proved to be one of the most lucrative markets for Doug's work as he has moved, cautiously, into his fifties. Fifteen years ago, he could still tour France, Germany and the UK, selling out the smaller venues, but these days it's just a date each for London and

Berlin, maybe a quick stop in Amsterdam, before heading south for the full Latin extravaganza. Even in Spain and Italy, though, most of the hardcore fans are the wrong side of forty – skinny men in ratty jackets and drainpipe jeans that, as they hear the twang of Doug's guitar, like to picture themselves as pool-playing 20-year-olds, bumming around some idealised bayou juke joint, giving the eye to a waitress in a low-cut top. When Judy's with Doug, she goes along with his gripes about his lack of female fans, but, secretly, she feels rather happy about it. She stills gets a buzz out of those dusty, romantic numbers – the ones that are about her, anyway, and not Arlene, Doug's first wife – when she's the only female in the room and it feels like his voice is an electric cable to her heart. When a member of the younger generation – a journalist, usually – does discover the Sipmeyer oeuvre, he is invariably male. 'Wow – we thought you'd be really old,' she told one twentysomething British interviewer, as Doug winced internally. 'Hey! Do you know any clubs over here? Places where we could go dancing, and people would be glad if Doug was there? We do still go dancing, you know! We're not *that* decrepit!' A reservoir of apparent calm beneath his aviator sunglasses, Doug didn't utter a word. He just rolled a cigarette and let her run a comb through his thinning salt-and-pepper shag.

To this day, Judy's mum and dad don't understand her relationship with Doug. He will forever be some Marlon Brando or James Dean rebel cliché to them, and she kind of likes that fact sometimes, but it can be difficult at Thanksgiving and Christmas, when there are plenty of awkward silences and the only way *really* to get Doug and her folks on the same planet is to sit him and her dad in front of the History Channel. When she talks about her duties as manager, PA and make-up artist, her mum looks at her as you might look at a five-year-old playing doctors and nurses. She doesn't need her to tell her they think she's bumming around, wasting her life, for her to know they say it behind her back. What they don't know is that, if she had a typical nine-to-five job, she wouldn't work half as hard as she does. What with maintaining the website, phoning forward to check that the TV in the hotel has a channel that is showing a rerun of *The Phil Silvers Show* and negotiating with shady promoters, it can all get a bit too much sometimes, and that was why, recently, she explained to Doug that she really had to start working five days a week, instead of seven. He looked up from his rare, original-edition DC comic and it was possible to see a hint of the snarl that had been knocked off the cover of *Rolling Stone* at the last minute by Aerosmith in 1978. 'Cool, Jude. Whatever you say,' he replied, before rejoining the Green Lantern on his adventures. Now, for two days in every week, the computer stays off and the phone remains unplugged – mostly. One of these days is a 'Judy and Doug Day', also known as a 'Candle Day', which will typically consist of a menu of massage, scented candles and 1950s sitcoms. The other is a 'Judy Day', and will normally involve her going to the local old people's home to read the residents' auras.

Today is supposed to be a Candle Day, but has turned into more of a Half-Candle Day for Judy, what with the calls to Spain and the (fifth) email to MTV to follow up the synopsis for her reality-TV show, *Loving Sipmeyer*. She won't bother Doug about any of this. Instead, she'll continue to cushion his landing on the runway to old age. After her fifth shout of 'Doug, bath's ready!' he will emerge, craggily, from their home cinema annexe, where he has been sitting beside their pet iguana, Idiot Wind, and watching an original print of the Birds. The next morning, when she wakes up, she will prop herself up on zillion-thread-count sheets and watch him sleeping in his hair mask for a few seconds, and what she will see is not a middle-aged grouch, but the twinkle-eyed bad boy she fell in love with – the one who, for her, was always that bit edgier than Springsteen and Petty. Then she will leap into action and fetch him his ice-cold morning Dr Pepper. As she does so, an urgent thought will occur to her. 'No, Sipmeyer,' she will say into the telephone a moment later. 'S-I-P-M-E-Y-E-R. I don't know if this is a good time to call, but I was wondering if you could tell me – do the rooms at your hotel come with fridges, or should we bring our own?'

THE BASS THUG

*For Paul, the car stereo is less an extra luxury than
an integral working part of the automobile itself.*

WHEN SUMMER KICKS in, it couldn't be more lovely in the valley:
the duck pond shimmering, the clematis blossoming in the courtyard
gardens, old Mr Cragwell with the ice-cream van that never dies.
'You might never need to go inside again in weather like this,' think
the older residents, but, come eight o'clock, they shuffle out of the
sun and lock the doors and windows – the luckier ones hiding behind
double glazing and enjoying the benefits of air conditioning, the
others sitting in wait, unable to settle until the first thump.

The only way that they rationalise the evil that hits the town on
these nights is by thinking about the days of their youth when they
scared their own elders with their Elvis, their Duane Eddy, their Hank

Marvin and their Beatles. But what they hear every Friday night between June and September seems like something else, a new level of incomprehensible musical uprising. It couldn't have anything to do with fun, really, *could* it? 'What kind of dark place does it come from – this need to pollute the atmosphere with these vibrations?' they think, as Paul does the first of his 36 circuits of the one-way system. He loves the looks that the ones brave enough to remain out on the street give him: somewhere between awe and incomprehension, he reckons. If he bothered to check his rear-view mirror more often, he'd see them speculating about the diminutive size of his manhood and just how much more bass he'd have to give his stereo before it made him spontaneously lose control of his bowels, but as it is he's too lost in the throb of DJ Godzilla and his own self-importance. The possibility that anyone could think he was anything less than cool in this machine and this Sergio Tacchini top is an equation one step beyond him.

For Paul, the car stereo is less an extra luxury than an integral working part of the automobile itself. Frequently, he's driven the Subaru Impreza without a properly functioning exhaust pipe, but, should one of his sub-woofers break, he wouldn't dream of even edging it out the drive. The last time one of his Wharfedales went bust, he borrowed his dad's Merc and proceeded to blow its weedy Blaupunkt. Caused a right laugh in Halford's car park, but the old boy wasn't best pleased when he got home and put him on all the crap roofing jobs the next day at work.

Working part-time for his dad in construction and still living at home is a convenient arrangement for Paul, who would be a likely contender for the title of Wales's Least Nuanced Twenty-Five-Year-Old, if they had awards for things like that. For two days a week, he will play Radio 1 at client-disturbing levels and use all his nepotistic craftiness to get a nearby chippie or tiler to shoulder his workload. This leaves plenty of time left over for ordering pizza, vegging in front of MTV Bass, overgelling his mini-mullet and impressing local sixth-formers with stories of the times (i.e. time) he used to organise (i.e. go to) illegal raves. As he lingers in the pay-and-display behind Domino's, girls in halter tops will gravitate towards him and away from the bad-postured boys in baseball caps they have arrived with. He will lean on the open door of the Impreza and nod at them, not saying much, but shouting 'Tuuune!' or forming a 'T' with his hands every time the DJ on Vibe FM plays an appalling remix of an old-skool rap tune that everyone will have forgotten by this time next summer.

If Paul had been the same age in 1982, the Impreza would have been a Capri and he would have been terrorising the neighbourhood with a *Dukes of Hazzard* horn, instead of a ringtone anthem sung by a tiny, grating cartoon character, and an ear stud would have been as ever present as his mobile phone. Would he have been more coherent? Unlikely. Still, the chances are that he would have formed a few normal sentences, instead of just a series of laddish, proudly working-class catchphrases. Even his dad – a former Capri man himself, before he joined the Federation of Master Builders and the local golf club – can't quite fathom what all this 'Come on!' and 'Get in!' business is all about, but it clearly means something to Paul and his mates, since it's all they ever say to one another. His only consolation, when he thinks about his hopes for Paul's future, is that his son's interests seem so fleeting. By next year, he'll perhaps be a bit calmer, have dropped the strange Welsh take on cockney rhyming slang, be ready to relinquish the alloy wheels. Maybe then they'll have The Talk – the one about taking a bigger role in the company. Of course, he should probably also say something about the driving and the bass and the nine points on his licence. But what can you do? You're only young once, aren't you? And, if your friends are a lot younger, at least it means you get a bit of skirt, doesn't it? That Debbie he brought home the other night: whew! He would have stepped forward and given him a thump on the back for that one himself, if he hadn't checked his bank statement a few minutes beforehand and seen just how much money he'd mysteriously donated to ringtone companies in the previous five weeks.

HEAT GIRL

When Nicola was still buying CDs, her typical purchase would be Robbie Williams. Now, she prefers reading about him.

IN THE RECEPTION of the anonymous image consultancy where Nicola works, the giant plasma-screen television is turned permanently to MTV, yet the sound is never on. 'Yeah, that is a bit weird, isn't it?' she said, when her friend Tara, who was meeting her for lunch, pointed this out. What Nicola didn't admit to Tara was that, despite having worked as a receptionist there for almost a year, she hadn't really noticed before. She's never been the most observant girl – once when she was on the phone to her mum in her bedroom and her mum asked her what colour her living room wall was, she had to go and check because she couldn't remember – and answering phones all day while watching those bright, brash images tends to send her into a trance.

Besides, it's not as if she didn't know all the tunes well enough already.

If the marketing board at a major record label were to encounter Nicola, who is 20, they could view her in one of two ways: either as a wet dream or an apocalyptic nightmare. On the one hand, an average week will find her consuming all their latest products voraciously and uncynically in all the places where they pump loudest. On the other hand, she hasn't bought a CD for four years. Why would she need to? She tries on a mock vintage T-shirt in Top Shop and hears some Madonna and Gwen Stefani. A couple of hours later she gets round to Tara's house, surfs through Sky Digital's ever-growing selection of music channels and catches the latest output by this month's most talked-about girl band while she's waiting for Tara to apply her fake tan. Then it's on to a nightclub in the centre of Manchester – usually the Funky Monkey night at the Ritz – where she gyrates to the output of the latest TV pop talent show winner, while an exhaust-fitter from Stockport tries to lick the back of her neck. The next morning it's back to work, and more songs – if not in the reception's speakers, then always in her head.

It would never occur to Nicola to pigeonhole herself as a musical being, and, when asked what she likes, she just says, 'Oh, you know, a bit of everything really,' which would almost certainly turn out to be a lie if she were ever to wander into a Tibetan throat-singing performance by mistake. She's usually too busy thinking about everyone else to be self-analytical. At school, she was regarded as a bit of a backstabber, but since the rise in outlets for celebrity news she's managed to channel her gossiping abilities into less destructive areas – to the immense relief of Tara, who's in the habit of having one-night stands with reserve-team professional footballers. During a typical lunch break at work, a watercress sandwich, the tabloids and *Heat* magazine keep Nicola more than occupied. If you want to be kept up to date on the developments of the latest on–off union of a pop star and children's TV presenter, she's your woman.

A few years ago, when Nicola was still buying CDs, her typical purchases would have included Robbie Williams. Now, she prefers reading about him to listening to him. She's very unnerved by what she's heard of his recent direction, but not quite as unnerved as when Girls Aloud just wanted to 'talk about their music' in *Heat* magazine, instead of about boob jobs, boyfriends or feuds. When her favourite girl-band singer changed her highlighted ponytail-and-quiff combination for a blunt fringe, Nicola did too, but she couldn't quite bring herself to follow suit fully and swap her hoop earrings for dangly neon plectrums. Nicola's style-consciousness snags her a good share of men, but none ever seem as sweet as her hero, David Beckham, and she can't help thinking that she'd meet a better class of bloke if her hair didn't keep sticking to her lip gloss.

Much of the time, Nicola struggles to find a bond with a man that stretches beyond the club and into the following week. She blames herself for this, wrongly, and secretly worries that she hasn't got one strong passion to share with people. What she doesn't see is the smouldering ardour that she carries with her everywhere she goes. Her love of music is so slinky, quick-moving and ego-free, it's sometimes invisible even to her. She can't be measured. The years come and go, the songs are loved, then forgotten. There are no concessions to future nostalgia. With the occasional exception of seventies disco, the past is uninteresting. Above Nicola in Rusholme lives a bloke called Tony, who collects bootlegs from post-punk era. Nicola calls him 'the Nerd'. Every so often, the pair leave the building at the same time, and say a distracted, muted hello. If you were watching them, you might look at Tony and think, 'That is a man who may well collect bootlegs from the post-punk era.' What you would probably not do is look at Nicola and think, 'There is a girl who loves music, who knows what she wants, who, just in the last week, has listened to twice as many songs as the man saying hello to her, and got much, much more out of them.' What you would probably think is, 'There is a girl who knows how to put herself together.' And quite possibly, 'I wonder where she got her handbag.'

THE NORTHERN SOUL SURVIVOR

Sometimes, Dougie will just walk into the room and zip down onto one hand, legs pumping in the air, blocking Gloria's view of Neighbours.

AFTER THE FINAL curtain falls, the crowd spills out into the street, and a quiet corner of Sheffield briefly comes alive with the clamour of cultural enthusiasm and the rustle of Sta-Press trousers. If you overlook the absence of Beano, who came to a sticky end a few years ago while bungee jumping in Australia, all the old gang are here, together for the first time since the Casino closed down, back in 1981: Shiner, Fat Man Thomas, Margie, Ian, Phil. Dougie doesn't know whether to laugh, cry or dance. If forced to choose, he'd probably go for the third option – throw some talc down, right here on the pavement, and wheel out the old 'spinning pliers' move – if he hadn't gone and twisted his ankle during yesterday's kick-boxing session.

'Fuckin' awesome!' seems to be the general verdict on the play, *Once Upon a Time in Wigan*, and most of the guys will see it at least one more time before its run comes to an end. Dougie particularly liked the little details: the permanently flooded toilets, the concept of records too rare actually to play. OK, so if he was being brutal, the acting might have left a little to be desired and he'd always thought plays and musicals were for queers up to this point, but who cares, because, well, 'It's Northern, intit?' and that's got to be good – always. That's the rule. The two green éclairs that he took beforehand can't have done any harm, either.

Dougie still does them all, of course: purple hearts, black bombers, blue donkeys. His kids know and don't seem to think there's anything remarkable about a 48-year-old man going to a holiday camp every couple of months and getting out of his face to the sound of the original version of 'Tainted Love'. Gloria and Dobie wouldn't want to join him themselves, of course, but they've never viewed him in the same way as the other kids in their class view their parents. He's just 'Dougie' to them, never 'Dad': a little bit weird, maybe, with his polo shirts, permanent aroma of Brut and habit of wearing bicycle clips indoors, but not sad. And, besides, it's not every kid who gets a lift to school in a souped-up Mustang. Moreover, unlike most dancing fathers of two, he can actually move. Sometimes, he'll just walk into the living room and zip down onto one hand, legs pumping in the air, blocking Gloria's view of *Neighbours*. It's sort of a ritual – no more unusual now than her mum's weekly nag about clearing the shopping away – and she puts up with it.

Secretly, Dougie's wife, Lesley, and friends – even the soul bunch – are amazed at how he keeps going. He tries to make sure that his pentathlons don't clash with the northern weekenders, and there's always time for a jog or a swim before he opens up the Army Surplus store in the morning. When he closes at 4.30, it's straight off to the squash court to meet Phil. He always worried that when he moved south, away from Wigan, to start his own business, the musical part of him would lack sustenance and die, but it never ceases to amaze him just how many people in South Yorkshire claim to have been there, at the hub, during the boom years of his favourite musical trend. Fittingly for Northern England's answer to Studio 54, the Casino has an almost endless supply of legends, myths and bullshit attached to it. He's often thought that, if everyone who'd told him that they were there in the late seventies was telling the truth, the queues for those waterlogged toilets would have been a hell of a lot longer than they really were. He can normally spot the pretenders straight away, but at least they're better than the non-believers and the ones who just can't see the point of the whole thing. Take that bloke from Lesley's office the other night at dinner, the one with the plastic genre dividers in his CD collection, who thought he was some kind of God-ordained archivist of black American music. 'But how can you claim that it's Northern Soul, when a lot of it was recorded in the American South?' he'd asked Dougie. Taking a deep breath, Dougie thought for a moment about going into detail – telling him that it's all about an attitude, a certain swagger, a religious belief in the infinite possibilities of Saturday night. In the end, though, he settled for a more basic explanation: 'It's just Northern, intit?'

THE INDIE KID

James likes to see himself as the hero of his own complex, sensitive art-house movie.

AT LUNCHTIME IN the university refectory, James flaps his *NME* about conspicuously, while the students who don't communicate entirely in band names speculate upon his hair from the other side of the room. Some say he lets it wash itself. Others suggest he uses a water-and-sugar mix on it. One thing is for certain: nobody wants to get too close to it. During an idle moment, one of his lecturers once mused to himself that it looked as if it had fallen on his head out of a tall tree, having been sculpted by a bored wood pigeon. But that 'lived-in' look is the result of hours of preening. Being the indiest person in your ziggurat is a full-time job.

The sixties architecture on campus is jaw-droppingly beautiful, but James doesn't notice: he's too busy archly evaluating the flyposters stuck to it. One day, he'll look back and realise just how lucky he was to be here. A direct product of the record collection of his older brother, he's always first to the Student Union box office when the gigs are announced and first backstage when they're over. It's not easy for him, studying in Norwich. He couldn't believe it during freshers' week when he realised that the city didn't have a branch of the hip retro clothes shop Pop Boutique. Where on earth is he expected to get his shirts from? Top Man? He'd much rather be somewhere cool, like Leeds or Sheffield, where the Strokes are more likely to play when they visit the UK. Nevertheless, in recent months he's managed to see Zaphod Beeblerocks, Buskowski and the Editors. You'd know this if you saw the cork noticeboard where he keeps his ticket stubs, in the hope that they will impress Myrtle, the panda-eyed girl who lives down the hall from him and acts depressed to get attention.

To those of his ilk one generation above him, James appears to be the Tony Soprano of indie rock music (albeit about seven stone lighter): they presume he has to be aware, as he goes about his day-to-day posturing, that he's come in at the cheap, corrupted end of a mysterious yet principled way of life, just before it dies. Indie, to them, is a vacuum-packed caricature of what it used to be. But does James know this? If so, he doesn't let on. Instead he likes to see himself as the hero of his own complex, sensitive art-house movie. He has only to take one glance in the mirror at himself in his tight black jeans, skinny tie and Converse baseball boots to be sure he's at the centre of something vital.

At university, James has four best friends – Dominic, Jem, Lester and Rich, who looks like the fat Hobbit from the *Lord of the Rings* movies – and he's pleased not only that they haven't quite tried to imitate his hairstyle but that they seem silently to acknowledge him as the group's leader. Although he would never let on, James has on the whole been pleasantly surprised by just how easy it has been to impress people since he started university. It's only a couple of years since he was a shy kid who was rubbish at football and went by the nickname 'Scroaty'. Now, he writes the word 'Cheese' on the back of a chair in a lecture theatre and senses that people look upon him as a surreal bohemian comic genius. Cool isn't a quality you can buy: either you've got it or you haven't. The other day, a Buddhist approached him in Norwich city centre, tried to sell him a self-realisation guide and said that he should be in a band. 'You see,' he thought to himself, 'people just *know*.'

There are those who don't understand James, of course – the mature students in his English lectures, for example. Or, rather, James *feels* they don't understand him, while they feel they understand him perfectly. They look at him, and they can see the ghost of a small child getting his lunchbox kicked around a playground. They also see a few years ahead, when the gap between self-image and reality will have narrowed for James, but perhaps not enough for him to deal with the real world of bills and mortgages and friends who no longer quote entire episodes of *The Office* back to one another verbatim. But what do they know? They probably don't even own one Franz Ferdinand CD between them (not, of course, that James thinks Franz Ferdinand are even *remotely* cool these days). The person James really wants to impress is Myrtle. Something about her hair tells him that she's just like him in every way. He'll approach her just as soon as he's finished reading *American Psycho*, which he feels will make him a Man of the World. For now he's playing things cool: making double sure to be talking loudly about a hip New York band or laughing with Dominic when she passes the two of them in the corridor, but simultaneously pretending not to notice her. Then, one day, he'll probably just climb in through the window of the room, sidle up to her, and say, quite simply, 'You're the one.' Just as Jim Morrison did to his girlfriend in that film about the Doors – the one his brother lent him.

THE LADY IN WAITING

Vicky still hopes that there is a place for her in the touring life of a loud, contemporary rock band.

'THERE ARE NO sexy men in this town!' Danny often hears Vicky complain after a night out. Still mindful of their one and only big argument – the one that ended up with Vicky storming out of the Bodleian Library and losing a shoe in the Thames – he will make the appropriate conciliatory noises, but the comment will secretly infuriate him. 'Oxford is full of intelligent, fit, colour co-ordinated young blokes!' he could point out. He could tell her that, at 28, perhaps it's time to compromise, time to realise that 'Does he own a guitar?' should not necessarily be the first question to ask yourself when a new romantic prospect knocks on your door. Experience, however, has told him that he would be wasting his time. Besides, he knows she's just spent a quarter of her monthly paycheque on that new pair of Marc Jacobs gold leather boots – the ones she's wearing over the grey Paper and Cloth jeans – and he wouldn't want them going astray.

'Am I cramping her style?' he worries. He hopes that the tight jeans and white T-shirt, the 'No, really, I'm just a friend!' body language are enough to tell prospective suitors that he bats for the other side, but – who knows? – someone might have mistaken them for a couple. Perhaps that's why her quota of skinny indie songwriter conquests has dwindled from the three or four a month that seemed to be the norm back in 1998 and 1999. He's started to feel old just recently in the queue outside Education, the Zodiac's rock and alternative night, and she must have felt it too. He thinks it's time to move on, give her some space, but he can't help feeling protective – or, at least, as protective as any five-foot-three man can feel of a woman who towers six inches above him – and he carries on cuddling her through the crying jags and sharing a taxi with her back to Cowley, even though, when you look on the map, you can see it's not even vaguely en route to his flat in Headington. 'It's always the cabbies that try it on with me,' she moans. 'Why can't Jim Morrison drive a taxi?' He gauges the redness of her face before deeming it safe to fire back with, 'Well, because he's dead, for one thing!'

Back in bed, Vicky flicks through a geological dictionary, confident in the knowledge that nobody will have yet plundered it for names for their rock offspring. She then dreams about Mick and Bianca's carefree wedding snaps, but with her head superimposed over Bianca's; about her hen night being featured as a four-page spread in *Elle* magazine; about an eventual move, with little Basalt and Gneiss, to a Georgian rectory in Buckinghamshire with picture windows draped in Pearl Lowe's dyed lace curtains. If she could just put herself in the right club at the right moment, she knows it's not all that much to ask. She thought she'd got the combination of time and place right in the Water Rats last week, but didn't realise that her overuse of eye contact and frequent lip licking had the effect of intimidating her prey somewhat. The deployment of Benefit's Bad Gal eyeliner and the ribbon-tie knickers hanging out of her jeans only succeeded in further overawing Benedict, the singer from the Concrete Noun. He'd only recently left his all-boys grammar school and wasn't used to having long conversations with girls, let alone ones this forward. Pinned behind a stack of flight cases, he'd just begun to feel three nervously downed pints of Foster's start to make some serious demands of his bladder when his tour manager, Charlie, had interrupted and led him out to the alley at the rear to 'look at that amp – that *very pretty* amp'. Vicky had waited an hour, but he'd never reappeared. After a delay in a tunnel somewhere beneath Edgware Road, she and Danny had ended up flat out, head to toe, on a bench at Paddington, having a delirious conversation about obsolete eighties chocolate bars. Danny headed straight to the museum to conduct the 9 am, but she missed her shift on the information desk at Borders bookstore and slept it off.

Still: the dream remains. Despite over a decade of first-hand evidence, she refuses to believe that it's only the quiet German documentary-film-maker girls who get the good-looking rock-star boyfriends. She still feels, in her heart of hearts, that hanging out near the entrance of the men's toilets is a failsafe pulling technique that gives her the edge over her peers. She still hopes that there is a place for her in the touring life of a loud, contemporary rock band. It would all be so much simpler if she submitted to the requests of her fellow staff at Borders. 'Fancy coming out to the cinema tonight?' they'll ask, and she'll kind of like the idea of seeing a restored print of *Vertigo* on the big screen, but then she'll ask herself, 'Who ever got together with anyone at the cinema?' She'll politely decline, instead ending up somewhere in Camden embroiled in a conversation with the drummer from a post-rock band about the way his album artwork is influenced by *Battleship Potemkin* – a conversation that will be rendered all the more faltering by the fact that she has seen neither the artwork nor the film.

Married college friends will attempt to fix her up with single acquaintances, but find themselves similarly rebuffed. 'But what about Jim, from the modern-art place? You liked him, didn't you?' Mary, her old gigging buddy, will ask, on the phone from her nineteenth-century farmhouse, from which she commutes to the London publishing house through whose ranks she is swiftly rising. 'Don't you just love his hair? Did you know he reads two books a week?' Vicky will make a noncommittal noise and explain that he was OK, but that she couldn't honestly ever see herself going out with someone who had never heard of Queens of the Stone Age. 'Don't feel sorry for me!' she'll snap, before Mary has even had chance to commiserate in the wake of another microrelationship that looked so bright and rock-and-roll at the outset, only to founder in a taxi somewhere between Jericho and the Oxford branch of All Bar One. A moment later, Mary will be making her excuses – 'I know, I know – some people work for a living, don't they?' Vicky will say sarcastically – and putting the phone down, but, 10 minutes later, she'll be on her laptop, using her last 10 minutes of freedom before five hungrily seized hours of sleep to register a new name at www.mysinglefriend.com. Forty minutes' drive away, Vicky rubs off her Bad Gal, puts on her house trousers and re-Blu-Tacks her *Faster, Pussycat! Kill! Kill!* poster to the living room wall. ('No, Mum,' she explained on the last parental visit, 'Russ Meyer did not degrade women! He empowered them!') She slips Destiny's Child's 'Survivor' into the CD player, but when it's finished she's very careful to put it back in a drawer in her bedroom, and not in the main CD rack, sandwiched between Depeche Mode and Devo. Word has it that Norbert from the Futility of Life and his new band, Manpon, are playing a secret gig in town tomorrow. And, while time has told her that you should take these guitarist types with a pinch of salt when they say 'I might swing by your place afterwards', you can never be too prepared.

THE EDUCATOR

*'Let's rock!' Simon told the head of year, Ms Prentice,
after his introductions to his fellow staff, and he meant it.*

IT IS FAIR to say that the second half of the nineties was not the most auspicious period of Simon's life. When he sees the first five years of the decade that defined him, he sees a pop-art explosion of colour. When he sees the subsequent five, there is only grey. One moment, it had been Blur's 'Boys and Girls', the loss (finally!) of his virginity, those mad, convoyed drives to the festivals, him in his Metro, the suspension sagging under the weight of guitars and sleeping bags, Degsy ahead in his parent-bought Clio – the spoilt bastard – almost missing the turning to Reading and barrelling across the grass verge next to the sliproad. Then – all the fun gone, in a flash. In fact, not even a flash. More like a smudge. No more gigs. All the old gang off somewhere happening and hallowed, completing their PhDs, or taking the first steps in unfathomable medically themed careers. Him back in Derby from university, stuck in his mum and dad's sixties bungalow, staring at a poster of Robin Williams in *Dead Poets Society*, trying to get into Blur's 'Beetlebum' (even Damon Albarn was depressed in the late nineties). The rejection letters. The factory work. His dad's voice echoing in his ears ('Not like in my day, when a bloody degree *meant* something!').

Everything started to turn around for Simon in 2001, after teacher-training college, when the governors at Challywell School decided that, in order to improve their dismal ratings in the league table, they would have to 'think outside the box'. Simon may not have been their first choice at another time, but his combination of floppy fringe and single ear stud and his tendency to use the word 'safe' in the context of 'fine' convinced them that they had found just the man to fill the opening in their RE and History Departments. Four weeks later, Simon pulled into the car park in the old Metro (missing a door panel now) and strolled confidently across to the staffroom, boom box in hand, 1994 Gibson Roy Smeck Stage Deluxe Reissue acoustic guitar across his back. Watching him keenly from the window of English Room 1, Mrs Croft found herself idly crimping her hair and checking her reflection for the first time since 1979.

'Let's rock!' Simon told the businesslike head of year, Ms Prentice, after his introductions to his fellow staff, and he meant it. A recent Year 11 lesson about World War One began with him sitting on his desk with his arms folded, nodding sombrely as his copy of the first Franz Ferdinand album played at length. He had originally meant to reach out to his pupils and make an important historical name stick in their heads, but, as is his wont, he got a bit carried away and started telling them about all the festivals he had been to. There was some consternation in the History Department later that year when mock GCSE papers were marked and it was found that many of the students seemed to be under the impression that the German Archduke's assassination took place in a waterlogged field two miles outside Leeds.

When Ms Prentice began to question his methods, he explained that his use of music was 'to really try to get through to these kids'. The reality is that most of the pupils in 10 and 11G are just grateful to get out of any proper work. Standing in the corridor and listening to the sound of Crosby, Stills and Nash's 'Teach Your Children' coming from Simon's classroom and unbridled chaos coming from those on either side, you might be inclined to see both sides of the argument. It is only in RE that the class tearaways will really attack Simon, as he attempts to use rock's most notorious religious conversions to explain the true nature of spirituality. A dunce like Carl Buncefield might make up his own lyrics to Depeche Mode's 'Personal Jesus' under his breath ('Your own … personal … teacher / someone to touch your hair / someone who's gay!') while Simon uses it to illustrate the multifaceted meanings of faith, but virtually everyone else knows it sure beats the time that Mrs Begley, the gym teacher, said, 'Today we're going to play some of *your* kind of music while we exercise' – and proceeded to insert Status Quo's 'Rockin' All Over the World' into the stereo. Later, after being caught stuffing snow down a member of Year 8's back, Buncefield will end up in detention with Simon, who will play him 'War (What Is It Good For?)' and 'Why Can't We Be Friends?'. For Carl, this will only be marginally less of a downer than the personal-development lesson Simon took where he attempted to use 'Up The Junction' and 'White Lines (Don't Do It)' as respective warnings about underage sex and drug use.

You might think that Simon would be worn out by a year of breaking up fights in the playground, experimenting with a variety of sensitive beards, dabbling in rudimentary drum'n'bass on the school music room's lone computer and lugging his instruments from classroom to classroom. The truth is that, come the end of term, nobody retains more energy. On the last day, he and the second coolest teacher in school – a bloke called Bob, who is the most popular PE instructor in school, by virtue of the fact that he is the only one who doesn't like to rub his knuckle into the kids' heads when they forget their kit – will don leather biker jackets and muddle through a song by Oasis in the main assembly hall. Afterwards, he will change into a sweatshirt which he will loudly refer to as a 'hoody'. That night, Bob will join him and a rare, visiting Degsy for a night out in Derby, and the three of them will end up in an Irish bar, where Simon's two friends will compete for his attention while he plays air guitar to 'The Boys Are Back in Town'. Bob and Degs will finally bond when they get into a fight with a weasel-like tyre fitter who is convinced they are trying it on with a barmaid he fancies. Simon will break the fight up and, as a result, win the interest of a student nurse called Natalie. 'Simon Redwood, BA, HMV, ELO,' he will say to her, proffering his hand. She won't know what the hell he is talking about, but, taken with his open smile and boyish manner, she will accompany him home. The next day he will drop her off at the hospital in the Metro and, even though she has showered scrupulously, she will spend the rest of the day wondering what that smell is that she is carrying around with her. Not unpleasant, it will remind her, at various points, of pencil erasers, straw, damp towels and a 1996 episode of the forgotten music TV show, *The White Room*.

THE ECO-ROCKER

Josh goes gregariously about the planet, thinly, and sometimes irritatingly, spreading his modernist hippie gospel.

JOSH'S FAMILY WORRIED when he announced he was going to England to study, but the truth was that he'd barely set foot into Heathrow, and already he was making friends. First it was the cyberpunk clubber types who sat across from him on the plane and invited him to that summer's Creamfields festival, then it was the girl in the taxi rank – sort of cute, in a wan, Eliza Dushku kind of way – who had her head buried in Eric Schlosser's *Fast Food Nation*. It has been the same for two years now. Having no fear of asking a complete stranger a moderately personal question has yielded a gradual accumulation of contacts, dictating that there is barely a European country that doesn't contain at least one couch where his indefatigable head is permanently welcome. It is also just perfect for his part-time job in Starbucks, where the combination of enquiries about the patrons' knitwear – 'That's not a Gap sweater, is it, by any chance?' – and kidding around with his fellow *barista*, Isla, makes the hours just fly by.

Usually, most of Josh's acquaintances will get together with him only fleetingly: they'll be busy completing their PhDs or doing night shifts in All Bar One, and he'll be keen to get to a cannabis-themed protest march or to see yet another friend he met on a train stranded on a track somewhere in the Austrian countryside or at a Donavon Frankenreiter gig. These relationships will be gratifyingly noncommittal, yet not without their share of intimacy. Hugs will be exchanged, keys will be left under plant pots, more profound character issues will be left unexplored. Just occasionally, though, matters will be given time to progress to a more involved level, and niggles will arise. A pair of laid-back yet not particularly eco-conscious student filmmakers in Amsterdam will come back to their flat and find the contents of their bin separated into four neat, labelled piles ('Aluminium', 'Garden Waste', 'Plastic' and 'Paper Products'). A goth in Durham will be surprised to find his anti-Jack Johnson stance quite so vehemently opposed. ('What? You don't like the Jack J? You've got to like the Jack J, man! I think you'd change your mind, if you listened a bit harder, and realised that he used recycled paper for his tour posters. I mean, shit, dude, he even used biodiesel in his tour bus!')

In this way, Josh goes gregariously about the planet, thinly, and sometimes irritatingly, spreading his modernist hippie gospel. When Malcolm Gladwell wrote about Connectors – the people whose social skills are vital in bringing a product or an idea to mass consciousness – in *The Tipping Point* (a book Josh has often cited as being one of his personal favourites, even though he has never got past page 98), he was talking about him. In ten years, he will find himself living with a stay-at-home wife and two kids in a house set 200 yards back from the road in a security-patrolled suburb of Washington, DC, receiving a six-figure salary, having been headhunted for a nebulous, complex-sounding position by a nebulous, clandestine corporation based in a monolithic glass building. For now, though, Josh doesn't even think about what he'll be doing in 12 months, never mind in a decade. How can you, when the ice caps are melting? And, sure, perhaps it's true that he won't form lasting bonds with the people who, alongside him, dressed up in elf and Santa costumes and sang anti-corporate Christmas carols in Oxford Street last December ('Oh little town of Oxford Street / How much we see thee lie / Telling us we need your plastic crap / And we must buy, buy, buy'), but, basically, who cares, when, for those eight hours, they all felt like environmentally aligned brothers and sisters of the closest sort? What a day *that* was! There aren't many people who could say that they managed to disrupt the Christmas grottos in three separate major department stores and still had time to get to the post office to airmail their family some bamboo-fibre bath towels and a natural-rubber yoga mat.

'But didn't that upset the little kiddies, when you kicked the plastic reindeer over?' asked his mum on the phone that night. He sighed in a way that said more about his disdain for his family's rampant consumerism than words ever could, began to mess about with a hacky sack he had found under the bed, and asked for her to put his sister on the line. Jenny told him that she'd been to the Body Shop website to look for that man's perfume he wanted but she couldn't find an aftershave called Acupuncture anywhere. 'No, you doofus. Not Acupuncture: *Activist*!' he corrected her. Then she asked him about those Coldplay tickets he'd promised to get her from the promoter he'd met last summer in Algeria. 'Don't worry, sis. I'm on it!' he said. 'Of course, you really should be going to see REM or the Beasties instead – don't you know Chris Martin's an eco-phoney who drives a four-by-four?' Having signed off with his favourite flippant, enthusiastic catchphrase, 'Cool beans!' – an expression known to cause a fair amount of confusion on the front counter at Starbucks – he switched on his iMac and proceeded to update his myspace.com profile for the third time that week. He noted with disappointment that there was just the one new post on the message board: 'Did you know that if everyone was to consume at the rate of the West we'd need five extra planets?' from tibetanmonkdude1. He added *March of the Penguins* to the sidebar list of his favourite films and *The Indispensable Chomsky* and *The Autobiography of Malcolm X* to his favourite books, and swapped his description of his ideal woman from 'Gwyneth Paltrow' to 'a younger Susan Sarandon'. Then he turned his attention to the picture at the top of the page – the one where he'd pointed the digital camera sideways on, 10 inches above his head, thus capturing a certain moodiness without quite obscuring the 'Certified Organic Beachwear' hemp leaf logo on his T-shirt. Perhaps it was time to relegate that to the 'Other Pics' section, and give precedence to the shot those scuba-diving freaks from treehugger.org took of him on the beach last year in Honolulu. 'That battered-straw-hat-and-sandals look,' he chuckled to himself. 'It never goes out of fashion, does it?'

THE RUDE GIRL

Tiffany really likes taking trips to Bluewater, where she once saw Jade Goody coming out of Baby Gap.

'JUST *WAIT*, WILL ya,' says Pudsy, carefully removing his fake-Burberry baseball cap from the coffee mug that he uses to keep the peak extra curvy. It's the morning of the monthly trip down south, and he'll probably make the rest of the Colchester crew miss the coach – again. While he preens for a little longer, Tiffany waits in the living room, fiddling with the screensaver on her new mobile, trying to decide which to go for: the fluorescent pink letters that say PORN STAR or the picture of Yogi Bear smoking a spliff. 'Fuckin' 'ell! Isn't it usually the girl who's supposed to keep everyone waiting?' she whispers to herself.

Down at the station, Jemma, Sarah, Asha, John and Figsy will all be waiting, Asha humming 'My Humps' by the Black-Eyed Peas while she applies her lipstick. They'll bitch about Pudsy behind his back but at no point will anyone suggest getting the coach without him. His pull on them is James Dean-like, but, later, as they hurtle through Chelmsford in an invisible yet palpable cloud of perfume and ringtones, fellow passengers will idly wonder what makes him the leader of the group. Is it that he was the first to get a Ms Dynamite album? Or is it just that way of mumbling he has, making his peers want to listen in closer? Probably the latter. Tiffany has had a silent chuckle to herself recently, as she's watched John – the baby of the group – try to adopt the same tone of speech, only to get comprehensively ignored.

Tiffany isn't quite looking forward to today's trip as much as her friends are, if she's being totally honest. It's one of their Little Trips and what she really likes are the Big Trips. A 'Little Trip' is what the Colchester posse call their excursions to Lakeside Thurrock shopping centre, near Dartford. A 'Big Trip' is what they call their less frequent days out to the more upmarket Bluewater complex, 30 miles or so further south. 'It's like a great massive … sort of temple fing,' she told her Aunt Fizzy, who wanted to know what Bluewater was like. 'All soofing and mellow and shit.' Asha claims she once saw 'Vicky' Beckham there, but the most famous person Tiffany has ever spotted was Jade Goody, coming out Baby Gap. Still – there's always hope.

On the way back, Sarah, Asha, Jemma and Tiffany will transfer the day's purchases to the large pink Jane Norman carrier bags that they take everywhere. Twenty minutes into the coach journey, things will tend to get rowdy, and the passengers with non-orange complexions will shuffle surreptitiously to the other end of the bus. Buoyed by his copy of the latest quasi-urban grime single, Pudsy will either sneakily get his stash of 'puff' out, or become unusually animated and start talking about some fight or other that he saw, or the time he spotted Mikey Carroll, the lottery lout, living it up down 'Colly Town C'. This will start Asha off on one of her stories about one of her uncles – probably the one who used to be a professional weightlifter and survives solely on Twix and protein drinks. She'll go on and on, a random stream of Essex consciousness, featuring 227 employments of the word 'like', until Tiff quotes that line from that funny movie: 'This one time, at band camp' – her way of telling Asha she's boring everyone. Asha will do that pouty thing that she probably thinks makes her look like Posh Spice, but Tiffany won't mind, so relieved will she be that Ash has stopped short of going into one of her spiels about Chris Moyles. You'd think he was one of her uncles as well, the way she goes on about the DJ, but Pudsy flies into a rage any time he comes on the radio. 'If I ever saw that fat fucker down HMV, I'd smack him,' he said, just last week. Tiffany could tell he was really mad, because he started fiddling with that 2-centimetre-thick neck chain that he's so mysterious about (he got it from Argos). She decided it wasn't the best time to ask why Moyles would be likely to be in HMV – particularly the Colchester branch. It's times like these when she wonders if Pudsy is going to be the future father of her child, after all. When it comes right down to it, she thinks Moyles is a bit of an annoying tosser as well, but you have to hand it to the guy: when it comes to new music, he really knows what he's talking about.

THE AUDIOPHILE

*Arjun dreams away whole Saturday afternoons in
Bang & Olufsen, comparing anti-vibration properties.*

GENTLY AND METHODICALLY, Arjun types in his code, and watches as the electronic gates open, his window down so he can hear that snapping sound he likes so much as they fold back on themselves and close: a snug fit reminding him how impregnable he feels here in Clarence Mount, one of Surrey's better class of late eighties-built gated communities. Bringing the BMW 7 Series to a halt, he goes through his routine. First, the placing of the spectacles neatly inside their case. Next, the retrieval of the reserve M&S shirt from the hanger on the back seat. Then, a final check of the hair – thinning now, almost to the point where the sebaceous cyst on his scalp is visible – in the wing mirror. Sure, there are more mirrors in the flat (16, to be exact) but what if Arjun bumps into the lady he likes from 13b in the corridor – the one he thinks looks a little like Calista Flockhart? One must always be prepared.

Once he is inside the front door and ensconced in the beigeness of his living room, the first task of the evening – even before he opens his first bottle of Michelob – is to check on the work of Lynette, the cleaning lady. Everything seems to be in order, with the exception of a slight smudge of lipstick on his 'Work Is For People Who Don't Play Golf' mug (how many times must he tell her, 'If you must drink, bring your own receptacles, Lynette'?). It's been almost three years now, but he still remembers the catastrophe that arose when her predecessor dusted a little too ferociously in the region of the stylus on his Nad turntable. Gives him shivers just thinking about it, although he wouldn't give that old Nad crudbox the time of the day now of course, not with his latest purchase shining in the corner: a Wilson Benesch Full Circle deck (five stars out of five in *What Hi-Fi* magazine), to fit with his Moon Eclipse CD player, Krell FPB amp and £300 Nordost Solo Wind speaker cables. One day he plans to retrieve his old vinyl albums from the storage container where they've been languishing since his divorce from Elaine, his former secretary, but he worries that his ultra-detailed system will only highlight their imperfections and put him in a testy mood.

When people who dislike and misunderstand modern minimalist living spaces try to imagine a modern minimalist living space, they think of a flat that looks like Arjun's. Desperately lacking in the feminine touch, it's a barren area, where no dirty crockery is left on display for longer than 1.7 minutes. The sole hints at a three-dimensional human presence come from the Ally McBeal poster on the wall of the kitchen-diner and the 27 CDs, filed in order of purchase, beneath it. To the left of this sits a small plastic case with the words 'Now Playing' stencilled on it – a present that Arjun can't bring himself to get rid of, given to him by an old flame, now married, whom he met in a chatroom frequented by crop-circle enthusiasts – and in this now sits the case to Jean-Michel Jarre's *Equinoxe*. Later, it might be replaced by *Wish You Were Here*, although, if he's being honest with himself, Arjun can never really understand its classic status. He prefers the later Pink Floyd stuff, dating from after Roger Waters left and the 'rough edges' came off the band. Contentedly unaware of Syd Barrett, he thinks their first album was *Dark Side of the Moon*.

Somewhere in the back of his mind, Arjun is aware that his domestic surroundings might not seem awfully nuanced for a man of 43, but at least his listening and grooming habits are. Since leaving Elaine, with her irksome dried flowers and messy DIY, he's plunged his head deeper into work, and it's had its benefits, as his motivational-speaking firm has gone from strength to strength. Now, when he hears about a new Calvin Klein aftershave, he need not hesitate before ordering it. Similarly, when he reads about push–pull EL34s and Mosfet outputs in monthly hi-fi publications, it's no longer the stuff of sonic pipedream, but of soothing, modular reality. Whole Saturday afternoons are now dreamed away in Bang & Olufsen, comparing anti-vibration properties. He's learned a lot, and as he listens to 'Parisian Walkways' by Gary Moore, he likes to think he can track the guitar solo all the way from the amp to the speakers. In the end, he's a commendably clean man and a highly organised one, but one whose 13-month break from non-onanistic sexual relations is starting to reveal itself.

THE OLD-SCHOOL GOTH

Dave had a go at being a punk, didn't like the bruises, and,
as a born outsider, simply moved on to the logical next genre.

BREATHING UNCOMFORTABLY THROUGH his nose in that way
that he always has done, but that seems that much more extreme since
his sixth nasal piercing, Dave moves instinctively towards his favourite
part of the bus. It is not just longing for his teenage years that makes
him favour the back seats: it's years of training in damage limitation.
You may not think it now, but there was a time when being a goth
would feel a bit like being the last surviving member of a tribe from a
South American rainforest – even in the North Midlands. It was a brief
time, admittedly, but it was a difficult one. You learned to put yourself
in the quiet places, to walk in the shadows.

All that has changed now, of course. Who runs from a goth, these days? It must be 10 years now since he's frightened a grandma, 15 since he's had to hear a townie shout, 'Oi! Dracula features!' When Dave started dressing all in black in the late eighties, he had no idea that he was signing up for a musical existence that would be undead in more ways than one, that seems to live outside fashion. The truth was, he'd had a go at being a punk, not liked the concomitant bruises very much, and, as a born outsider, simply moved on to the logical next genre. These days, he'll tell you that the reason he got into goth was that he saw Ian Astbury on the *Whistle Test*, and went out and bought the Cult's *Love* album. If he's more truthful, he would say that a larger turning point in his musical sensibility was the day when one of his mates lent him a copy of the preternaturally camp, ultra-soft porn film *Elvira: Mistress of the Dark* and he became obsessed with the star's lustrous black hair and plunging necklines.

When Dave was 16, his best friend, who was called Nigel but changed his name to Trevirion for reasons known only to himself, got on the local TV news because he slept in a coffin. The coffin was actually an ottoman that had had been painted black and had its top removed, but Trevirion didn't tell the local news crew that. Dave has never done anything quite so extreme to show commitment to his tribe, but he did use to disrupt family barbecues by getting black nail varnish in the dessert and once wore his sunglasses to a game of indoor five-a-side football in an attempt to look like Wayne Hussey from the Mission. He doesn't know Trevirion any more, but thought he once saw him queuing up to see *How to Lose a Guy in Ten Days*.

Until a few years ago, Dave lived in Nottingham, but has now settled down with his girlfriend, Angelica – imagine a plumper Siouxsie Sioux with a penchant for Sock Shop – in her native Leeds. He feels, in goth terms, Leeds is 'the town Nottingham aspires to be'. The couple met at a goth weekender in Whitby, where the organisers were raising money for a cat-rescue society. They shop for 'bits and bobs' at Pentagram, an alternative herbal and magick shop in Wakefield, but buy stuff from Accessorize, too – or at least Angelica does, while Dave checks his eyeliner in the mirror. They still go out clubbing once or twice a week – to Black Veil at the Adelphi, Black Sheep at Bar Phono or Carpe Noctum over in Bradford – and for the most part are reassured by the fact that plenty of people there are as old as they are. Most of the friends they meet at these clubs are obsessed with cats, too, and this is usually what they end the night talking about. Angelica wants a Persian, but Dave's mum worries about Dave being allergic to cat hair.

When he's out on the town, Dave dons the trusty Doc Martens he bought from the Derby branch of Jonathan James in 1994, black drainpipe jeans and a tight, frilly white shirt, a bit like the one Tom Cruise wore in *Interview with the Vampire* – though he insists that's not why he wears it. To whiten his face, he uses Hypersmooth Foundation in Porcelain by Max Factor or Aqua Powder Whitening Cleanser by Dior. Last November, he spent 300 quid on getting his hair straightened. He and Stacey could upgrade from the terraced house they bought for sixty thousand before the last boom, but they'd rather spend their money on CDs and 'beauty'. He knows he's vain, but is less ashamed about it than many of his friends from the non-goth world. That said, he tones the look down for his day job at the DSS: the Fields of the Nephilim T-shirt stays at home. His workmates can still tell he's a goth. They used to act a bit scared – he is six foot three with a portentous sickle-shaped nose – but now they kid around with him and call him 'Vlad', though always with an air of confused respect. He likes this respect. He also likes the fact that he doesn't get as much aggro as some of his colleagues do from some of the DSS's more unhinged patrons, but he has no idea why this is.

Does he miss the days when dressing the way he did seemed special, when it was something that bonded him as fiercely with his peers as it alienated him from the other 98 per cent of the music-loving world? He is not sure. Certainly, he'll sneer gently when he sees a photograph of a facile, fluffy celeb wearing a Cure T-shirt (he never thought they were a proper goth band, anyway), and notices that the kids who hang around on the steps across the road from his office have ditched their skateboards and now wear lots of dark eyeliner, long black jackets, and talk about how cool Brandon Lee was in *The Crow*. Dave's not certain that these kids see the intrinsic values of his tribe in quite the same way he did. But, then, he's not sure he does, either. It's been a long time since he hung around in a graveyard or read any H.P. Lovecraft; he hasn't listened to the Sisters of Mercy's *Floodland* since his mate Big Mike played a tape of it on the way to a psychic fair in 1998, and most of his friends are anything but macabre. He even caught himself crying for joy the other day, while watching the bit where Xander stops Willow ending the world in *Buffy the Vampire Slayer*. You'd probably hesitate before putting forward the theory while he was wearing his favourite six-inch-soled boots, but you could say that, for Dave, being an Old-Skool Goth has simply become a foolproof, reliable route to a social life among people whose natures are just as gentle as his.

THE SUPERDEALER

*How does Elfie come up with the goods again and again,
in this age when the democracy of eBay prevails?*

WHAT IS IT, that magical thing that makes records sound so
seductive in Elfie's flat? Is it his ancient turntable, its perspex cover
dust-etched from countless hastily discarded drinks and the
powdery residue of a hundred joints, its diamond stylus
indefatigable? Is it a certain kind of aural hoodoo or sonic feng shui,
a particular speak-friendly furniture arrangement? Nobody is quite
sure, but everybody is agreed on one thing: no LP that you buy from
Elfie's place ever sounds quite as beguiling when you get it home. It's
not that his steadfast clientele – an assortment of DJs, musical
excavators, overpaid number crunchers and know-it-all music

journalists with too much time on their hands – are disappointed with their original Badfingers, their Tim Buckleys, their Charlie and Inez Foxxes. The thrill of the thick gatefold sleeve, the toasty crackle of needle on plastic and the sense of owning a small piece of history – it all lives on, long after the cash has been coyly exchanged. Nonetheless, soon a craving kicks in for a trip back to that living room high above Primrose Hill, with its atmosphere of joss and paused time. In this way, it is ensured that Elfie's astronomical quarterly council tax payment is never late, that his 12-year-old twins, Charlotte and Fred, will not be taken out of one of north-west London's more exclusive private schools, and that his French wife, Magali, can continue to supply homemade cushions and papier-mâché animals to a local craft shop at a pace that is sedate, rather than breakneck.

Elfie's mortgage is a thing of distant memory now, having been taken out at a time when wealthy relatives of Magali were dying off at an alarmingly swift rate and finding mint copies of the first three Scott Walker albums didn't quite so closely resemble the quest for the Holy Grail. Nonetheless, there is still a certain amount of speculation among his peers regarding how he stays solvent. How does he come up with the goods again and again, in this age when the democracy of eBay prevails, levelling the playing field for several thousand prevaricating, snaggle-toothed vinyl dictators? This age when it seems as if every charity shop has been pillaged? Nobody knows, and they are damn sure Elfie won't tell them. What they do know is that, every half a year or so, he will leave the country. Nobody knows exactly where he goes – most presume America – but, when they picture the place, they picture a land of treasure-packed lofts. For the next two months, radio silence will prevail; the pager that Elfie persists in using in stubborn preference to a mobile phone will go unanswered; frantic email requests for the first Shocking Blue album will fall into the void. The word, when it comes, will arrive out of nowhere, at the moment when it is least expected. It may be a voicemail, or it may be an email, delivered in the dead of night, but the message will always be to the point – 'Give me a call when you feel like spending some money' – and those on the receiving end will know exactly what it will mean. It will mean that one of the most dangerous rooms known to the bank account of Anally Retentive Man will be full, once again, with unknowable riches.

Not for Elfie the scrum of the rare vinyl auction or the elegiac ritual of the village hall record fair, with its reused Budgens carrier bags, optimistically overstocked Elton John sections and half-cocked concessions to the age of the digital reissue. Not for him the faint disillusionment of the open-air market stall, where 'mint' serves less as a description of an item's condition and more as a warning of the half-sucked confection to be found welded to it. By confining his trade to his own home and buying his furniture in the golden age of the Habitat sofa, he has provided that rarest of things: an environment where people can buy records without feeling paranoid, harried, cold or bullied.

With his bendy-tree outlook on life, Elfie contributes to the calming aura in no small way. One of perhaps a dozen men in the Western world over the age of 50 who can make the wearing of a baseball cap look dignified, he will never raise his voice, even when showing enthusiasm for an overlooked early Motown album by Kiki Dee or a mod seven-inch of £500-plus in value. 'Quality, this one, mate,' he will say, in the voice of a stoner Roland Rat, as he expertly blows some fluff from the grooves. When he thrusts a copy of Keef Hartley's *Overdog* album into your hands, he won't say, 'You have to buy this!' since he knows he doesn't need to. The unruffled, erudite look in his eyes is confirmation enough. Sometimes, a client will tell him a story from the cut-throat outside world of his profession – the anecdote, for example, about the lady in the record shop in Sheffield who doesn't sell anything for over £3.50, who banned the dealer with the twitchy eye from rifling through her stock, after she realised he was selling it for profits of up to 25 per cent on Amazon marketplace.

Elfie won't say a word in response. He will just smile in the manner of someone who has a little secret. Then, noticing that his guest's mug is empty, he will repair to the kitchen to root out some green tea and boil his fifth kettle of the day.

Still more of an air of mystery remains about Elfie's past. Every so often he will talk about the time when he worked in a real record shop. He will do this in the manner of a famous method actor recalling his old, starving days on the theatre circuit. Sometimes, he will talk about 'my mate who's in this band' and it will be only five or ten minutes into the conversation when you will realise he is talking about one of the most renowned hit makers of the sixties or seventies. The complete refusal to namedrop only adds to the mystique. 'Surely,' his clients muse, 'he must have been more than just a buyer and seller of records at some point in the past. But what?' Elfie remains tight-lipped. He may let his vinyl junkies sit in his living room for lengthy periods of time, he may let them blast out an Iron Butterfly album while Charlotte tries to do her homework in the adjoining room, but he will never let them inside his head. It would be a deal breaker, for one thing. He knows that, were they to get too close, their lust for his stock would dwindle. So, instead, he will let them invade his space, and he will play the groovy, placid host and endure their regurgitated factoids about the making of Love's *Forever Changes* and the death of Tim Hardin, and he will take their money. Then, a few weeks later, when all that remains on the shelf is a couple of Mamas and Papas albums and a dented copy of *Abbey Road*, he and Magali will leave the kids at his mum's place and, in the company of a couple of hippie friends from the old days, take a plane to San Francisco, hire a car and drive down the coast to a log cabin not far outside Salinas. No records will be purchased on this trip. Maybe the two couples will drop a couple of tabs of something on the way. Then, when just the faintest embers glow in the fireplace and the night air has reached its coolest and a bat flaps its wings outside the cabin, he will reach across to Magali beneath the duvet and whisper four little words: 'Hold me. I'm scared.'

THE NU-METAL KID

Just a year ago, Siobhan was dressing like Lindsay Lohan and belting out Alanis Morissette's 'Ironic' at the end-of-term concert.

'GOSH! SHE'S CERTAINLY got a mighty voice!' exclaims Sue, handing Siobhan back one of the headphones from her personal CD player. Slouched against the wall outside the agricultural museum, in the Derbyshire countryside, Siobhan fixes her mum with a doleful stare from beneath a lock of jet-black, dark-blue-streaked hair.

It's the second time that she's given her the chance to listen to her self-made compilation CD, *Eat Shit, Corporate Rock Children*, and the second time she has been mistaken about the gender of the lead singer of one of her favourite bands. Sue always seems enthusiastic, which is more than Siobhan can say for her dad, Alistair, who was boring everyone with his Smiths CDs on the way up here, but it's at times like these that Siobhan wonders just how genuine she's being.

'I mean, it's basically an empirical impossibility,' she thinks to herself. 'If she can't even tell that Billy Corgan is a man, how can she really tell that his band, the Smashing Pumpkins, were one of the main progenitors of all that is vital and heavy in modern hard rock?' She doesn't quite know what 'empirical' means, but she uses it a lot these days. It's one of her favourite words, along with 'sensibility', 'dichotomy' and 'faggot'.

Today is something of a bargain between Siobhan and her parents: in return for not moaning while spending an afternoon examining seventeenth-century ploughs and millstones, she will be permitted to go to the Evanescence concert in London tomorrow, accompanied – though not all the way to the venue's entrance, obviously – by Sue.

On the way here, her mum joked about the prospect of heading along to a club on her own while the concert is taking place, and Siobhan couldn't quite tell whether she was serious or not. It strikes her as ridiculous, Sue at a club at the age of 38, and, dwelling on the concept, she conjures up an image of awkward businessmen and women in suits and bowler hats, awkwardly apologising for moshing into one another. 'So gay!' she thinks to herself, but doesn't say it, since her dad never believes her when she tells him that, among her immediate social circle, the word means 'lame', not 'homosexual'.

Alistair and Sue are amazed at how their little girl has changed: it doesn't seem so long ago that she was a cuddly, if slightly precocious, prepubescent who regularly wrote verbose, somewhat right-wing letters to broadsheet newspapers about bad language on television. Now it's all GM foods this and Tibetan freedom fighters that. It's got to the point where they can't decide what was better: the half-informed vegan rage, or the prissy young fogeyism.

By her own admission, Siobhan really has come on a lot recently, in matters of taste and opinion. Just a year ago, she was dressing like Lindsay Lohan and belting out Alanis Morissette's 'Ironic' at the end-of-term concert, not realising that, by standing on stage looking no older than her 13 ³/₄ years and singing the line 'It's meeting the man of my dreams, then meeting his beautiful wife', she was testing the groovy liberal values of a couple of hundred corduroy-wearing parents. That seems like 'forever ago' to her. Now she's much more edgy and clued up, and her heroine is Amy Lee from Evanescence, whose blank, Bride-of-Dracula demeanour she adopts in double biology, when Mr Horning harangues her for holding her hand in the flame of a Bunsen burner. Other icons include Staind, Spineshank, the Lost Prophets and Korn, the last of whom she has been known to refer to as 'kick-ass gods who put metal back on the map' despite having heard only one of their songs.

Does she feel like a rebel? In the right environment, yes. It's sort of tough to view yourself as a wild child, when your mum recently borrowed a Tool album from you and commented on its heaviosity, but at school she's the one the alternative girls look up to: the first to learn the bass and read Naomi Klein's *No Logo*. Of course, it's hard work staying ahead, particularly now that 48 per cent of Western teenagers listen to nu-metal, and changing her hair colour once a fortnight can be a pain, but what's the alternative? Listening to Britney and going to see the latest teen flick? Hanging out with the dreaded school 'posse', led by Melanie Deakes, that royal bitch who once said Siobhan smelled 'of death' in front of Rob Harrison, the coolest guitarist in school? No thanks. Sure, with a quick trip to New Look and Toni and Guy, she could be like them, too, and make them snipe and gasp at just how pretty she really is. But she's got foresight, and knows it's better to stay true to yourself. In just a couple of years, she'll be at college, and that's the time when the doomy, unassuming girls come into their own and get the best-looking guys. It's a period she's prepared thoroughly for, even to the point of choosing her subjects: sociology and media studies. She just wishes it weren't so far away. Sometimes, the thought that she'll have to wait all that time to write an essay on the legalisation of marijuana seems almost unbearable.

RAVE MOM

There is a story behind Nancy's bellybutton piercing that only a couple of people are allowed to know.

THE IMPORTANT THING that you have to know about Nancy is that she may have moved to Brighton, but she did it early – 'before it became London-on-Sea'. She wants you to be well aware of this, and feels it is an important part of who she is, so she will usually tell you about it within three or four minutes of having met you. She and her boyfriend, Leo, have two children, Honey and Sentinel, and their two-bedroom flat on the outskirts of Hove is starting to feel a little small for the four of them, but they're delaying the inevitable move, since Leo is sure that, if they keep applying for long enough, they'll make the shortlist to be featured as house hunters on Channel 4's *Location, Location, Location*. Nancy thinks that this is just because Leo fancies Kirsty Allsopp, the presenter, but kind of likes the idea too. Anybody who's anybody has been on a property programme these days, haven't they?

When she was a fledgling raver at comprehensive school in the mid-eighties, a lot of kids in Nancy's class wanted to be graphic designers without really knowing what it meant. She was the one who went on to actually carry the ambition through (though she's still not entirely sure she knows what being a graphic designer means). She likes to think she has an instinctive knack for colour co-ordination, but most of her friends – all of whom Nancy refers to in a high-pitched voice as 'darlin' – secretly think the yellow and navy-blue paintwork of her living room is ghastly. It reminds the ones who have known Nancy longest of the dungarees she used to wear in the late eighties.

Nancy doesn't wear her bright-yellow dungarees any more. Like her old hooded tops and love beads and the 'Jackson Pollock' cardigan she knitted herself in 1988, they languish at the back of her wardrobe, stashed for a 'rainy day' that Leo hopes never comes. These days, she prefers Earl jeans and Birkenstocks or old-school Adidas trainers combined with designer child-size T-shirts which show off her bellybutton piercing, behind which there is a story that only a couple of people are allowed to know. She is determined, in a laid-back kind of way, to stay true to her roots as an original member of the Rave Generation. 'Having kids hasn't changed me, darlin',' she always says. She still listens to Orbital and the Shamen, but she keeps up, too: her last few purchases from Virgin include the last Goldfrapp album and the Ministry of Sound's *Ibiza Sunsets* compilation. In 10 years, when Sentinel and Honey are hitting their teens, she hopes she will be the mum that their friends think of as the hippest. Will she still be doing drugs by then? Possibly. Most people find it hard to gauge whether she does them now. Her overuse of the words 'cool' and 'chilled' suggests she does. That said, anyone who rooted through her shopping bag at the weekend – stuffed with organic vegetables after one of her ritual visits to Borough Market –

might imagine that she's too much of a health freak to pollute her body with evil chemicals. Nancy still goes to a few clubs. Generally, though, the portion of her life that she once spent in mindless pursuit of the groove is now spent sipping fruit crushes and echinacea tea while discussing her metabolism with close friends.

Nancy is light of hair colour and spirit, but is just classy enough not actually to say 'blonde!' as a self-directed insult. Her friends – most of whom do PR for overpriced brands of alcohol and skincare products – think of her as an enigma: a stand-up girl who would never let you down but whom they can't ever quite get as close to as they'd like. Her ex-boyfriends – all of whom she has stayed in touch with – feel very much the same. Everything in Nancy's immediate orbit – from the scummy, crime-ridden area of east London she used to live in to her favourite minimalist furniture shop – is always 'fantastic' or 'wicked', but what does she really think? Even in the old days, mashed out of her brain in Ibiza, her surface warmth seemed only a couple of layers thick, before you got to something as potentially icy as her favourite Nordic chill-out album.

Despite this – or perhaps because of it – Nancy has never fallen out with anyone in a big way. On the occasions when she does go out, she's still always on the guest list, and nobody knows quite how she does it. She claims to have known Meg Matthews in the good old days, but it seems weird that all Nancy's best friends have known Nancy since the good old days too, yet they somehow never managed to bump into the one-time Mrs Noel Gallagher. Nancy is better-looking than Meg, but somehow not quite striking enough for anyone to develop an infatuation with her – even the placid Leo. She's faintly aware of this, and it worries her, as does what lies beneath her Touche Éclat, which she's been reapplying excessively for years. When people talk about 30 as the new 20, they're talking about her. Actually, she's 34, but that's OK, isn't it? She's the last person who should be fretting about being old and boring, right? On her last trip out to stock up on nappies, she also purchased the latest Blue States CD and a Smeg fridge.

THE ZEN DRIFTER

Like a lot of session guys, Adam knows where the bodies are buried.

'YOU CAN RELY on Adam,' said the former member of the semi-famous band – the one who hit hard times when their manager became the singer's boyfriend – to the member of the other semi-famous band (the one who hit hard times when their guitarist began to cough up blood just outside Reading). 'He's a pro.' Now, arriving at the venue, that professionalism begins to show, in its own quiet way. The lead singer has lost his voice, the drummer has discovered that the tour manager has left most of the band's percussion instruments on a pavement in Glasgow, and the bassist just stared at the same page of his 1978 *Beano* annual all the way from Scotch

Corner to Stoke-on-Trent, but Adam is a model of calm as he strolls into the venue and places his Rickenbacker neatly behind an amp, at a distance from his bandmates' instruments that manages to make a definite statement without being conspicuous. The one member of the group who has put something more substantial than two double brandies and a packet of sherbet lemons in his stomach today, he takes a clear-eyed view of what is in front of him. It is a scene he's evaluated a thousand times before: the goateed bassist from tonight's support group repeatedly, deafeningly, playing the riff to 'Have Love Will Travel', a journalist standing nervously in the wings (probably local, judging by the flapping notebook), a couple of men in Metallica T-shirts milling around, scratching their ribs. 'Would most people go to gigs, if they knew the full, disconsolate horror of sound checks?' he wonders.

There was a time that this kind of thing would get to him. There would be a point, back when he was on the road with his first couple of bands – when they really were *his* bands – when that grey mid-tour feeling, that feeling that every mixing desk was the same and one riff was just like any another, would make him feel as if every creative endeavour in the world was ultimately pointless and there was nothing over the rainbow. Some might say that the difference between Old Adam and New Adam is only that Old Adam felt it, while New Adam knows it. But with that knowing has come acceptance. And with that acceptance has come an epiphany: if you never got too attached to this rock-and-roll game, you could do quite well out of it. You might even come out of it vaguely sane.

'You should be fronting Oasis or Primal Scream!' Adam's friends – not his best friends (they all like cricket, and don't really know much about music) – tell him. 'Not bad,' shrugs each new employer, bitterly, as, in a matter of seconds, he learns the tunes they have slaved over for hours. Adam just lets the tiniest grin escape the corner of his mouth, as if making some profound, internal decision (he had just made up his mind to have Thai for dinner that night, and not Japanese). Even his most prominent paymasters can't help finding themselves swayed by his easy style and encyclopedic rock knowledge. One day, he will turn up at the studio and find one of them sporting a new feather cut or paisley neckerchief remarkably similar to his own. Another time, having finished transforming one of their leaden, jelly-mould rock songs into a slightly less leaden mid-level chart hit, he will watch a documentary about their troubled personal life and notice a copy of, say, Patti Smith's *Horses* placed out on a table. 'He thought she was a fucking tennis player until I bought him that!' he will say to himself, sigh, and change the channel to check the score between Glamorgan and Somerset. The secret will remain safe – just like the one about the crafters of a well-known eighties duet whom he caught making the beast with two backs over a legendary central London mixing desk. Like a lot of session guys, Adam knows where the bodies are buried. If only journalists bothered to talk to him, he could help them unlock the key to Rock and Roll Babylon, but they rarely do. They can tell he's removed from proceedings, a distant stepchild in the intense, four-way marriage that is the typical touring rock band. Or perhaps it's just the ever-present copy of *The Tao of Cricket* that puts them off.

Adam is one of the most misunderstood bit players in the music industry. He is the kind of man who, when he has a slight headache and closes his eyes for a section and holds his forehead, gets people mistakenly believing he's in the middle of some advanced meditation ritual. People think he's deep, detached and scarred. In reality, he's just someone who has found a way successfully to separate work from his private life and take the time to enjoy the spoils that his musical talent gives him, unhassled. Nobody knows what happened to him to put paid to his restless ambition to be 'the next Keith Richards'. Friends from his second band, Acker, recall his walking off the tour bus just outside Las Vegas, then not seeing him again for six months. The Adam who returned was somehow stiller, quieter, but with a surprising number of worry lines around the eyes. His Mancunian accent had gained a mid-Atlantic quality ('Tranatlancunian!' as Chris, Acker's clownish, hyperactive drummer, put it). Common speculation has it that he busked for a while, met a Mexican prostitute, and got involved in some 'bad black-magic shit' somewhere in South America. The truth is that, while he did play bottleneck outside the New Orleans Jazz Festival for a while, he soon got a bit bored and boarded a boat to Barbados, where an uncle he hadn't seen since childhood had relocated in the early eighties. He stayed there for the whole summer. The worry lines are actually just the result of spending too much time outdoors without suntan lotion, watching the local self-sufficient test matches. He would tell you this if you asked him, but people never do. Instead, they stand at a safe distance and feel sorry for him. 'Bloody waste of talent, that,' they will say, as they see him in the studio, sheepily playing along to a former boy-band star's thinly disguised musical tirade about how annoying it is that the paparazzi aren't more co-operative with his publicity needs. 'He could have been a modern-day Jimmy Page.' But wasn't Jimmy Page happier and more balanced when he was a jobbing session musician? Didn't all the bad stuff – the summoning of the beast, the unspeakable acts involving groupies and their shoes – start to happen when he actually started his own band? Sure, Adam would like to write his own 'Stairway to Heaven', but then there'd just be the inevitable explosion of ego, the fallings-out, the drug abuse, the sleepless nights, the stalkers. Say what you like about the perks of that lifestyle, it does not create the sort of environment where it's easy to watch the Ashes uninterrupted.